Praise for *Success Ag...*

"The story of Teach First is of an improbable dream that has become a remarkable reality; a thousand graduates making a vast impact on some of the most needy schools in Britain."
Jon Snow, *Channel 4 News*

"The remarkable, gripping and often funny story of a young American on a personal crusade; to succeed at mission impossible, to break down Britain's chronic educational divide."
Dr Anthony Seldon, master of Wellington College and Tony Blair biographer

"Teach First is an inspiration to everyone concerned with social change; that it really is possible to build a movement of people who want to help every child reach their potential."
Camila Batmanghelidjh, founder of Kids Company

"Teach First is changing the face of English education – and English society. It has made teaching in challenging state schools not only a job, but a mission, for many of the highest achieving graduates, the sort who would never have dreamed of going into teaching a decade ago. Brett Wigdortz's story is passionate, honest, inspiring and very moving. It is a testament to vision and leadership, full of optimism and faith in the power of the human spirit to create the world anew."
Lord Adonis, former education minister

"Teach First is great. Everyone should do it."
Jeremy Paxman, BBC *Newsnight*

"Teach First has been a transformational force in schools, and a major lever in raising achievement by pupils. This is the extraordinary story of how one man's belief that change is possible helped change the education landscape in Britain."
Sally Coates, headteacher, Burlington Danes Academy, London

"Brett's insight is that strong leadership can change lives. He brought a business approach to the world of British education that has the potential to change it forever. Every business leader and entrepreneur can learn from his experience."
Joseph W. Saunders, chairman and chief executive Visa Inc.

"Teach First is one of those rare things – a big idea that changes society... This book is a must-read for those who want to learn how they too can lead real change in the world."
Jim O'Neill, chairman of Goldman Sachs Asset Management

"The Teach First graduates who worked in both my schools made a huge difference to the progress of the schools and the life chances of the young people in them. This has been and continues to be a brilliant initiative."
Joan McVittie, president of the Association of School and College Leaders and head of Woodside High

"Teach First is a programme that recognises our shared responsibility for raising standards in schools, combining business, the voluntary sector and schools themselves."
David Cameron, Prime Minister

"Teach First is a brilliant charity that does so much to address educational disadvantage and inequality in this country."
Nick Clegg, Deputy Prime Minister

"Teach First has played a crucial role in attracting the brightest and the best into teaching, raising the status of the profession and improving the educational outcomes for children in some of our most deprived communities in our country."
Ed Miliband MP

"The wonderful thing is that there have been so many teachers who have come from university, who would have gone into something else, who have seen the point of Teach First. It shows just what an enormous movement this has become. To see the difference it's making to children's lives is, I think, of enormous encouragement. Above all else I think it's an investment in the future."
HRH The Prince of Wales

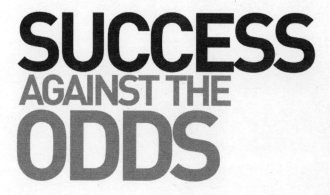

SUCCESS
AGAINST THE
ODDS

SUCCESS
AGAINST THE
ODDS

**Five lessons
in how to achieve
the impossible:
the story of
Teach First**

BRETT WIGDORTZ

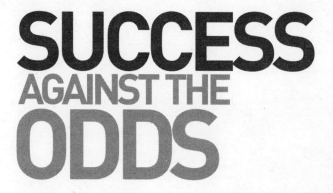

Published in 2012 by Short Books

Short Books
3A Exmouth House
Pine Street
EC1R 0JH

10 9 8 7 6 5 4 3 2 1

A CIP catalogue record for this book
is available from the British Library.

ISBN 978-1-78072-130-9

Printed in Great Britain by CPI Group (UK) Ltd.
Croydon, CR0 4YY

Only those who risk going too far can possibly find out how far one can go.

T.S. Eliot

Dedicated to the memory of my father,
Larry Wigdortz, who taught me a sense of humour
and belief in the goodness of people that has enabled
me to look past the valleys of death and see the hills of
happiness in every situation.

CONTENTS

Foreword

I am delighted as chair of Teach First in our tenth anniversary year to write a foreword in support of Brett's book about the founding and development of Teach First. Many 'how to' books have been written by entrepreneurs but few have been written about the challenges for social entrepreneurs seeking to change entrenched social norms and succeeding against the odds. Brett's single-minded determination and hard won experience on how to garner the support and change mindsets makes compelling reading.

Failure was never far away and entrenched prejudices were at times overwhelming. Memories fade, of course, as some who were the most sceptical now remind us of their early support. Success has many midwives while failure is an orphan! Brett would be the first to acknowledge that this has not been achieved alone and the support of those who we like to call our "Founding Ambassadors" was crucial – those individuals whose support, courage and belief in those earliest days helped to align the stars and get the enterprise off the runway. They and many others have played a crucial role in backing Teach First and the radical innovations it proposed.

My earliest personal recollection was of a summer's afternoon at Highgrove where the Prince of Wales, President of Business in the Community, had invited headteachers and business leaders to report back on a successful twinning programme called Partners in Leadership. The Prince of Wales remarked, rather sharply, that although he could see benefits for business people – in getting a window on a world they only dawningly understood – and there was anecdotal evidence of benefits for headteachers, he proposed a proper evaluation which should ask what headteachers really wanted from business. The following day, Business in the Community's Education Leadership Team met – including some senior business leaders and David Hart of the National Association of Head Teachers.

The Prince's proposal was made and Ian Davis supportively agreed to put a McKinsey team on to it which turned out to include one Brett Wigdortz. People like Jo Owen, Rona Kiley, John May and John Dunford among many others also played a crucial role in the early days. For all entrepreneurs the key test is the first investor and that came from Sir George Iacobescu of Canary Wharf Group, who gave us the first £25,000, and helped to trigger, with Rona and Stephen O'Brien from London First, the business support which has made so much difference. Jim O'Neill and Sir Peter Lampl, who has done so much through the Sutton Trust to tackle educational disadvantage, were key early supporters. Lord Andrew Adonis, who played a vital role as a key political support who unblocked the blocks, also deserves a very special mention.

Having been on the Board of Teach First for the last nine years, and Chairman for the last six, I know that there are many hundreds of people who deserve all of our gratitude for helping to make Teach First a reality, civil servants like Ralph Tabberer who had the creativity to change the rules, educationalists like Professor Tim Brighouse, Professor John

Moss, James Learmonth and Professor Sonia Blandford who backed their innovative instincts, and not least the dozens of dedicated members of our trustee and advisory boards, the hundreds of headteachers who have partnered with us and the thousands of graduates from university campuses across the UK who decided to change their mindset and come and teach first.

None of this would have happened, if Brett had not resigned from McKinsey (with Nicole's willing support), focused and determined to make this dream a reality. His dream was to persuade the most sought after graduates to teach in the least sought after schools – and then to take on the mission of tackling educational disadvantage for the rest of their leadership lives. This book tells the tale of how a social entrepreneur, supported by an outstandingly talented staff team, has begun to achieve that goal and thereby transformed the life chances of young people as a result.

1 August, 2012

Dame Julia Cleverdon DVCO, CBE
Chair of Teach First and Vice-President of Business in the Community

INTRODUCTION

Prison is bad. But this was worse.

At least in prison there is a sense of order. Here, there was little order, and not much evidence of control. Chris, one of the employees, showed me round. His face wore the cares of a thousand conflicts. His eyes were always glancing over my shoulder, looking around for the next crisis, the next abuse, the next problem.

I had only been in Britain for a few months and was visiting one of the largest secondary schools in west London, but this did not feel like a school. Long corridors, tense faces, low level disruption and a feeling of marking time without much to show for it. The man showing me around reminded me of a tired warden, hoping to keep any disturbances low level and avoid trouble until he could retire. "There haven't been any problems today," he said hopefully. It was a sad, depressing place. What made it even more so was that the "inmates" were all children and they hadn't done anything wrong – except to be unlucky enough to live in the wrong catchment area of London.

I was in the school to get some ideas for a *pro-bono* education project my management consultancy employer had assigned me on. It was the first time in my life I had been in a British school and it didn't look anything like what I had imagined. In reality it seemed more like a prison, a prison of low expectations.

My first impression was how sad the entire place felt. The stench of apathy hung over the entire building – no smiles, no aspiration, no structure. It was obvious when walking around that the real victims were the young people in the school who were being failed by the adults responsible for their care.

I got dropped off at an English class where the students argued and talked over each other about everything except the writing lesson the teacher was valiantly trying to explain. The bell rang and I asked one of the pupils what he had learned. He laughed, "It's just a waste of time." I had trouble not agreeing with him.

As the students filed out, I asked the teacher what his goals were for the class.

"We want to keep them out of trouble."

"Out of trouble?" I asked.

"Yes, if they leave here at sixteen without any problems and we keep them off the street, then we've done our job. You can't expect too much from these kids. Many of their parents aren't even literate." He shrugged. "The best thing you guys can do is send us some money and stay out of our way."

He wandered down the corridor and left me to let myself out.

Even now, eleven years later, I'll never forget that meeting and my simplistic thoughts as I stepped outside, totally deflated. This isn't fair. These children deserve better. How can someone already be giving up on kids who are only twelve years old when it's their job to change things?

* * *

Any journey has to start somewhere. This journey started in Chris's school. That visit was the call to arms that I needed. I had been working on a project on how businesses could support schools in challenging circumstances in London. We prided ourselves on the intellectual rigour of our analysis. Looking at the data, it was obvious that most schools with children from low-income communities were not succeeding, but they were only numbers on a page, no more real than any other statistical analysis. I needed more than analysis to move to action. Seeing is believing, and realising how some of the young people were being left out of their only opportunity for advancement was shocking.

Luckily, this was only part of the picture. Not all schools were failing their students. In fact, some were inspirational. And, even in the most challenged places, there were islands of remarkable professionals devoting themselves to raising the aspirations and attainment of their pupils. What some of them were achieving was truly moving. I especially remember a visit to a school in South London, trudging through the grey London mist past boarded-up shops and 1960s concrete housing estates. The school itself was nothing much to look at until one stepped inside, where the headteacher's brisk optimism was apparent from the moment I arrived. The cheery signs on the walls, the receptionist greeting visitors, the teachers and the pupils all united by their pursuit of success and learning. There was a purpose to the place – a common vision. The school was succeeding with their students. The head had ten minutes, sat me down in a corner of her office and recounted in bullet points what she was looking for from business partnerships – work experience, interview training, IT support. As I scribbled furiously she closed with her most important request. "Tell them to stop poaching the best graduates!" she ordered. "We need them. They don't!" I laughed at her comments. She gave me what I'm sure was her patented headteacher scowl for naughty children. She was deadly serious. I wrote it down. She sent me on my way.

There weren't enough places like this and they seemed so isolated. The successes of some only served in my mind to underline the failure of most. If students in one school could do well, why couldn't those from similar backgrounds in another? To me, it seemed a failure of leadership – not just the school leadership or classroom leadership, but also wider societal leadership. Why weren't more people doing something to change this situation? If hundreds of thousands of children in Britain were being starved of food, no one would allow it. How could anyone find this starving of opportunity acceptable?

Education is the most crucial way for young people to make the most of their individual talent to enable them to lead a successful life. As well as a moral imperative, it is also an economic one. The British economy has no room for an uneducated workforce. Poor education for some drains resources from all. Almost all of the people who took part in the 2011 riots were united by the lack of an effective education, with only 11% having achieved the five or more GCSE grades A*– C, including English and Maths, that are the minimum expectations of most students in the English education system.[1]

Quite simply, in twenty-first-century Britain, a great education is the most important way for a child to unlock a better future. The lack of this opportunity for some of our youngsters is a modern day version of the ancient scourge of slavery or feudalism where a person's life opportunities were dependent on the parents they were born to. If we no longer live in a society where it is considered acceptable for freedom to be rationed by status at birth, then this simply has to be the most important issue of our time. Luckily, if there is unanimity around any issue it is this – everyone deserves an excellent education. Everyone needs an excellent education. This is one of society's greatest responsibilities to every one of its young people. No one would openly disagree.

At least that is the theory.

The reality is quite different. For it remains the case that the greatest determinant of a child's educational success continues to be how wealthy their parents are. This correlation in Britain is among the strongest in the developed world. A recent OECD study showed that parental income in Britain has over one and a half times the impact on their children's incomes compared with Canada, Germany and Sweden, a situation that seems positively feudal.[2] The waste that underlines this is immense and frightening.

1. *After the Riots: The Final Report of the Riots, Communities and Victims Panels, 2012.*

2. OECD, 'Economic Policy Reforms: Going for Growth' 2010.

It's time to man the barricades. It doesn't have to be this way.

Study after study, expert after expert, common sense observation after common sense observation all show the same thing.

An excellent education is the result of teachers who demonstrate excellent classroom leadership, enabled by effective school and wider societal leadership. These are the key ingredients of an excellent education, which we all know can have a major impact in changing young people's lives. They are not the only things that matter – there are many other factors that contribute to a child's educational success, including their early years and out of school experience. However, it is indisputable that no education system, no school and no classroom can be better than the adults who lead them.

Everyone from Secretaries of Education to my six-year-old daughter (who will follow her teacher to the ends of the earth) intuitively understands this.

In what other public policy issue is there so much agreement around the basic principles of success?

Yet, in 2001, with some notable exceptions, why wasn't it happening? Why weren't enough of the most able, motivated and inspirational leaders in the country choosing to go and teach in a school in challenging circumstances?

Let me rephrase that. It wasn't that they were considering teaching in a challenging school, carefully weighing the pros and cons and deciding to be an accountant instead. Most were considering teaching in a challenging school the same way they were considering being a Martian surveyor or an underwater sculptor. In other words, it wasn't something entering their consciousness. To give one example, in 2002, less than 3% of all Russell Group (recognised as the top British research universities) graduates went on to apply for any sort of teaching qualification course at all directly after university.[3] As one head of career services at a top university sniffed to me "Our graduates aren't really interested in those sort of jobs. They're looking for something with more prestige."

More prestige. Why would anyone think that sitting in an office pouring over spread sheets was prestigious, while leading young people and changing lives wasn't?

However, priorities can change.

In the autumn of 2001, having been in Britain for only a few months, I wrote the business plan for the charity that would become Teach First. By autumn 2012, we would become the largest graduate recruiter in the country, working with over 500 schools, tens of thousands of young people, dozens of universities and businesses and all the national political parties to help make change happen. The greatest leadership lesson I've learned over the past decade is that the future doesn't have to be like the present, just like the present isn't always like the past. Change really can happen.

At its heart, the idea of Teach First was very simple and consisted of three stages. First, it involved attracting the best graduates in the country to join the programme. Not best as in the best grades, or best in terms of university background, but best in terms of leadership potential. This had to be highly selective.

3. Institute for Public Policy Research, 2002, "Male Teachers Vital to Teaching Shortage."

Then, they would complete a training programme, but it wouldn't be just any programme. It would start with something that would feel like a boot camp, a basic training that would be short, sharp and tough with high expectations and quick skills transfer. It would be residential. That was crucial. They would live together and learn together and begin to function as a cohort together. They would become outraged about this problem together and they would bond together in this adversity. They would teach for a minimum fixed period of time – a two-year commitment similar to most graduate employers' fast-track training schemes. They would work with schools of education, other teachers and leaders inside and outside of their schools, through continuous training during the two years to learn how to be highly effective. What was crucial was that they wouldn't be teaching assistants, they would have to be fully responsible for their classrooms. They would do this in schools in the most challenging circumstances where they could potentially make the greatest impact.

They would be expected to be leaders. Classroom leaders from the start – working with their students to prove the maxim that true leadership is leading people to a place they need to get to when they themselves don't believe they can get there. They would be well supported during the two years by the best leadership training from all partners available.

However, two years of teaching from each graduate wouldn't be sufficient to upend an entrenched national injustice. They would have to lead change beyond this period. Because society had to change. During their two years, they would become so outraged, so bonded and so sure of the potential of their pupils that they would never stop fighting for them. This led to the third part of the plan. They would have to become a movement of leaders dedicated to this for life. Some would continue as excellent teachers, others as school leaders, while others still would be supported to make this change happen through roles in business, policy-making, charities and their own enterprises.

In some ways it was a deliberate sleight of hand. No pressure, just a two-year commitment. In reality, I was convinced that the graduates would make it a lifetime one.

They would join other great teachers, school leaders, charity heads, business champions and policy influencers outside of Teach First to become the most powerful movement in the country, helping to lead a revolution that would ensure all young people in Britain got the excellent and life-changing education they needed and deserved.

I naively started to show the business plan around. This, I thought, would be the easy bit. People would immediately embrace this idea and take it forward.

The more people I showed it to, the more problems people saw. My colleagues laughed. "We don't do revolutions in this country mate," one sniggered. A few were indulgently supportive and for them, I will be eternally grateful. However, most smiled at my innocence and then ripped into the idea and its many, many flaws. The most obvious one was that I really didn't understand Britain. Most observers with any knowledge of what would be involved felt that this would be too difficult to get started. Where would the money come from? Entrenched bureaucracies would need to change. It would require an unprecedented and impossible degree of cooperation and coordination between the private and public sectors, between schools, teacher trainers, graduates, unions, businesses and government. To achieve this would take a huge amount of personal Commitment – which I now realise was my first real lesson in leadership.

Next, in the unlikely event that it did get started, just about everyone believed that it would be best run by civil servants in government, or at the very least by an expert in British education. In other words, not me. This made complete sense, but for some reason common sense was not correct in this instance. For this project to be successful, it needed to be led from the heart – sometimes an emotional connection can prove more powerful than decades of experience. This led me to my second leadership lesson: the importance of believing in yourself, taking on feedback, constantly learning and working with real Integrity.

The graduates. It was explained to me that there was a huge difference from other countries. I kept on hearing the same refrain, "British graduates aren't idealistic enough to want to teach those children". Many experts in the graduate psyche believed that there was none of the romanticism or civic mindedness that's present in other countries. Instead, with a booming economy, there were many other opportunities for them to follow the siren call of the Porsche in the City rather than work in what some people unfortunately felt was a discredited profession, teaching unruly teenagers in hoodies. I didn't really believe this needed to be the case and so learned a powerful leadership lesson on the importance of high standards in attracting and motivating great people. It taught me the value of a focus on Excellence to make change happen.

Many experts also believed that even if this project did get off the ground and managed to find a few interested souls to sign up to it, they wouldn't have much of an impact. It was felt that it takes years for a teacher to effect change. Anyway, how would they be trained? As one official explained to me, "It takes sixty-three standards to become a teacher and there is no way that those can be taught at speed. For instance, have you thought through how number 2.3 or 4.1 will be taught through your model? It will be impossible!" She was right. It would have been impossible for us to do this alone. Luckily we made some friends. But first I had to learn the leadership lesson of Collaboration – that by working together you can achieve much more and begin to break down "impossible" barriers.

Finally, it took years for many observers, and even many of our closest supporters, to really understand the most powerful part of the concept. This wasn't a teacher recruitment or training programme. It was about growing a long-term movement of leaders dedicated to overturning a national injustice. As more than one colleague sniffed: "We don't 'do' movements in Britain." The idea of thousands of people working together towards a common vision seemed untenable. This led to the most crucial lesson of all – the importance of everyone uniting within a Leadership mentality. The young people we are working for will only have the opportunities they need if everyone takes personal responsibility for leading the change necessary to make that happen. None of us individually are responsible for this problem, but all of us can be responsible for the solution. You can be a spectator and be concerned about the situation, or you can be a leader and take responsibility. Our teachers and their colleagues needed to be leaders. As more and more individuals felt a sense of responsibility to solve this issue, it would unleash the incredible power to make real societal change possible.

These five leadership lessons – the importance of living the values of Commitment, Integrity, Excellence, Collaboration and Leadership – were painfully learned, but have already started to enable many of the young people we work with, and their schools, to succeed against the odds.

The past eleven years have taught me that things change all the time. However, in 2001 it wasn't just Britain that had to change – I had to change. I was twenty-eight years old, I had no public policy experience, no experience in education, had never led anything before, had never managed anyone before, and found myself in a strange country, without any professional network. I was the least likely person to help make this change happen.

Michael

Michael is a sweet fifteen-year-old Geordie lad who is constantly smiling from the moment he enters class until the moment he leaves. Unfortunately, that is almost all he does as he is largely unable to speak. He has a severe mental illness and is barely able to communicate. He was unable to get a place in a Special School and the headteacher could not find a more appropriate place for him in this school, so he is in our teacher's bottom set English class filled with large, scary looking boys described by other teachers in the school as having severe behaviour difficulties. Our teacher was given this class because he is the newest member of staff and so received the timetable that no one else wanted. He views this challenge as an opportunity, setting up a rota for different children to be responsible for helping Michael each day, both in class and during lunch and breaks. After a few initial complaints, every boy starts to look forward to this duty. Our teacher builds a culture of peer support in the classroom that demands everyone helps each other to succeed and no one is allowed to fall behind. It is one of the most joyful and supportive, but also purposeful environments I have ever seen. It is the only place in the school where Michael feels connected and for the first time in his life develops basic verbal skills. All of the other children in the class go from being deemed the "worst of the worst" in the school to starting to show some success, with almost every one of them gaining a "C" or above in their English GCSEs, though none started the year expecting to. Most of them volunteer to support Michael the following year.

1

"This will never get started."
The Value of Commitment

As I sat in one of the small interview rooms at McKinsey & Company's London offices off Piccadilly Circus, desperately trying to spin my meagre experience, the manager of the project, John Kirkpatrick, looked back and forth between me and my CV with a wary eye. "So, basically, your only experience in the education field, besides going to school yourself, is that your mum teaches at a high school? Why exactly are you applying for this project?"

I'm sure that if I had told him the truth, I would never have been selected. I was the employee of last resort.

This was back in 2001, and I was applying to get on to the *pro bono* education project that would eventually take me to Chris's school. I desperately needed to get selected. The system at McKinsey requires that junior employees like myself apply for and get selected on to different projects within our own chosen specialist area in order to build up a portfolio of experience. If you go too long without this, it threatens your place in the firm.

My background had been in financial services, but these projects were in short supply in late 2001. As a result, I had applied for half a dozen projects simultaneously in a number of different fields. I was up for anything.

My career so far had been peripatetic and lacking in any obvious structure or plan beyond trying to see as much of the world as possible. I grew up in a small suburban town on the New Jersey shore, about fifty miles south of New York City, next to Bruce Springsteen's "Hometown" of Asbury Park.

I went to the local school with the same group of kids from the age of five to eighteen. About half the graduates moved on to university and I was one of them, going out of state to study at the University of Richmond, a small liberal-arts college in Virginia. During my final year at university I applied for dozens of opportunities with the main criterion being that they took me to the most exotic locale possible.

The winner turned out to be a two-year position at a Honolulu-based think-tank, called the East-West Center. They offered free lodging, airfare, tuition for a Masters in Economics degree at the University of Hawaii and about $600 a month. I jumped at it.

During my time there, I began to focus on Indonesian issues and, as a result, found myself in Jakarta in 1997 when revolution broke out around me. The Asian economic crisis and an angry middle class stirred a popular revolt against the thirty-one-year reign of strong-man Suharto. Soon, the impossible happened and he was overthrown, leading to rapid changes as a free press started to proliferate and democratic elections were held. I ended up staying in the region, working as a freelance journalist for about a year, writing about some of the massive changes occurring around me. That period left me with a deep realisation of how even the most calcified of systems can quickly transform beyond all recognition.

Feeling that my thirst for adventure and excitement was finally sated, I moved back to the United States. At a loss on what to do next, in the summer of 1998 I ended up back in my old summer jobs, working as a valet car parker and lifeguard at an upmarket beach club and living with my parents in New Jersey – a situation none of us found particularly appealing.

One particular low-point was when I applied for the head lifeguard position at the beach club and was told that I didn't have enough leadership skills or experience to hold onto such a role. Probably the true nadir of my career, though, was when I was fired from a chicken delivery job at "Cluck-U" fried chicken shack because I took too long on my routes, getting lost while driving in those pre-GPS days. After two nights, I was told to hang up my chicken hat.

Luckily, this was in the midst of the dot-com boom and even someone who couldn't deliver chicken could get a job. I used my Indonesian experience to get a temporary role as head of Southeast Asian policy and business programmes at the Asia Society, a non-profit organisation based in New York that focused on increasing ties with Asia. A few months later, I applied for and, after one day of eight back-to-back interviews, received an offer as a junior associate with McKinsey & Company's new Southeast

Asian offices – based in Jakarta. At the time, I only had a very vague notion of what a management consultant did and still remember a congratulatory conversation with my grandmother that didn't help. "It sounds like a great job. What is it you will do exactly?"

"Well, I will work with banks and other businesses to advise them on how they can work more effectively and efficiently."

Pause.

"But you've never worked in a bank or a business."

"No, but the idea is that we use special systems and ways of thinking about problems to help them."

Long pause as she tries to think how she's going to explain this to her bridge group.

"As long as someone is paying you for this I guess it sounds like a splendid job." She didn't sound convinced and I suppose neither was I.

Yet, for over two years, I worked with banks and other financial institutions throughout Southeast Asia, in Singapore, Manila, Jakarta and Kuala Lumpur, helping them build insurance units, hold onto high-net worth customers, and engage in the chest-thumping "War For Talent", which helped them attract and retain the best employees to increase their profitability. I enjoyed the work and was competent in it, but felt like I was missing a level of meaning that I wanted. Crucially, I learned the skill of condensing complex ideas into simple structures, and how to convince experienced bankers that I knew what I was talking about. Only my grandmother remained unconvinced.

In early 2001, I sat down with my manager who asked

me about my career plans. We agreed that financial services were core to my future and that I was developing a useful "knowledge spike" in this area that could help me progress at "The Firm" (as McKinsey is known). He suggested that the best way for me to develop my knowledge in this area would be to spend a year in Europe working with some clients in more developed markets, before returning to Asia in a more advanced role. There was a placement opportunity in Stockholm that he thought would be perfect for me. Having never lived in Europe before and still young and unattached enough to be able to get on a plane and move continents at a moment's notice, I agreed. Two days before my flight, I received a call. Could I go to London instead? The office there had more vacancies than the Nordic branch. My SAS ticket was returned and a BA flight duly purchased. Just like that, my life changed completely.

I landed in Heathrow in February 2001 caught up in the city's Cool Britannia shine, having gone through a short cultural induction course with fifteen other international recruits. (Best question on the Introduction to British Life FAQ we received – "What's the difference between a Knight and a Lord?")

After being duly acculturated, the fifteen of us were given an office in London and waited to be accepted onto a project. We then waited some more. And some more. As it happened, we landed at the exact same moment that Britain entered into a short recession and projects dried up. As the newbies, we were bottom of the group to be selected. Things started to get desperate. I knew the situation was bad when I got jealous of one of my colleagues who was accepted onto a six month energy project in northern Siberia. Instead I was sent to work with a bank in Manila for three months and, after I returned, bounced between a few different short-term projects. By September, I knew that I needed to get a serious project under my belt in order to feel that my time in the UK had been meaningful – and in order to go back to Southeast Asia and spin my mostly underemployed year into a professional development experience.

It looked like this education project would be my chance. In addition, it was a subject that I was personally interested in. I come from a family of educators – my mother has been in the classroom for over forty years and my aunts, uncles, cousins and brother could probably run a school between them. Schools and teaching were the daily conversation around the dinner table. Beyond that, I had no specialist knowledge or experience, but the more I thought about it, the more the idea of looking into what businesses could do to improve education in low-income London schools really appealed to me. I managed to convince John and somehow he selected me onto the project team and we started in early September 2001.

The origin of this project only became clear much later. During the summer of 2001, the Prince of Wales, in his position as President of the business membership organisation Business in the Community (BitC), hosted business leaders involved in a twinning initiative with headteachers called Partners in Leadership at a Highgrove reception.

The discussion ranged over issues that concerned him about the performance of inner-city London schools and whether business was doing enough to make a real difference.

He felt that inner-city London schools were not doing as well as they needed to. "What" he asked, "were the causes of these poor results? Could British businesses do anything to help turn this around?" Everyone looked at each other uncomfortably. There were no easy answers. After a bit of an awkward silence and, possibly, with a element of dread about what they would need to commit to, all eyes turned to Ian Davis, who was then in charge of the London office of McKinsey & Company. Ian agreed to put a team of consultants together to look at the issue – *pro bono*. They would report back to BitC and a sister business membership organisation, London First. These recommendations would then make their way up to His Royal Highness.

The work was due to run from September to December 2001. A team of four consultants was put together, including John and myself. During the first two months, we researched the issue and tried to understand the problem. I spent two weeks examining the results of hundreds of school inspection reports to find statistical trends and correlations. Unsurprisingly, they showed what any headteacher or educational observer could have said – there were schools with great results in London (among the best in the world) and schools with poor results in London (among the worst in the developed world). And the greatest determinant of whether a school had great or poor results was the background of the students in the school, which was heavily segregated by income.

HOW TO LOOK AT A PROBLEM WITHOUT "BOILING THE OCEAN"

Like most management consultancies, McKinsey & Co. works with organisations across the private, public and social sectors and across a wide range of industries to help their clients make lasting and substantial improvements in their performance.

As part of this, they often commit some resources every year to non-fee paying, or *pro bono* projects, one of which led to the creation of Teach First.

Depending on the needs of the client, teams of varying sizes, expertise and experience are put together and assigned to a project, the manager and more junior consultants (of which I was one) are committed to the project on a full-time basis, while the leadership typically share their time across a few clients.

The project is tightly planned and structured at the outset in full collaboration with the client team. The first step is to define the problem; teams usually fill in a statement worksheet which is shared with the client and articulates the basic problem to be solved. This includes answering questions about the context of the problem, the relevant stakeholders and processes that need to be taken into account, criteria for success, scope of the solution space (i.e., what will not be covered during the project) and any barriers to impact.

The next step is to simplify the problem by focusing on the key issues using a technique that is called a "logic tree" – this sets out all of the possible solutions to the problem and also helps to divide the work into work streams that members of the team will lead on. The most common approach is to find mutually exclusive and collectively exhaustive (MECE) ideas to make up the branches of the tree. Once the logic tree is complete it is important to prioritise its components according to pre-determined criteria to ensure the team's effort is focused on activity that adds the most value to the organisation.

One example could be: how can the company close a £100 million profitability gap in two years and create a sustainable platform for the future? The tree might then have three elements: increase operational profit; pursue external diversification; sell company and reinvest funds.

The 80:20 rule is often quoted, meaning that 80% of the impact is typically delivered by 20% of the effort – thus emphasising the importance of retaining focus on those elements that will make the largest contribution to solving the problem rather than analysing absolutely everything, which is often referred to dismissively as "boiling the ocean".

Simultaneously, in order to ensure buy-in, it is important to understand the key stakeholders. Each project involves a kick-off meeting with the internal team and the client. Teams are usually based at the client site for a big part of the working week to ensure day-to-day collaboration, continuous sharing of knowledge as well as reinforce the idea that consultants and clients are working together towards the same set of goals.

The meat of the study is then the problem-solving. Each member of the team will lead a workstream independently but the team will also get together to "problem-solve" critical questions and synthesise findings across workstreams. The team also leverages experts in the relevant industry and/or function from across the world to ensure they are up to speed with the latest knowledge on the specific problem being addressed.

Finally, projects culminate with a set of recommendations, usually shared with the CEO in partnership with the client team.

As one of the most junior members of the team, my role was to do some of the lower level work, and I was sent out to visit some schools in challenging circumstances and interview employees to find out what they thought the business sector could do to help. At first, it didn't go very well. During most of my visits there was a distinct mistrust and lack of imagination about what businesses could provide and rightly so. Schools had experienced an overload of initiatives and weren't interested in more. Many of the business people they had interacted with before had been patronising, and relatively clueless – believing themselves experts because of memories of their own privileged schooling many decades earlier. I was visiting from a different world and many of those I met with preferred to close the school gates and their classroom doors and keep the outside world out, often for understandable reasons.

Yet, over time, as I saw the young people to whom the data alluded first hand, my understanding of the issue moved from my head to my heart. This is when it really hit me. I was used to working with numbers, not children, and had never seen places like this before outside of low-income communities in some of the much poorer countries of Southeast Asia. It wasn't just that these young people were failing (though they were) – it was clear that they were *being* failed. At first glance, many of the buildings were crumbling (though over the past ten years, most of the worst facilities have been rebuilt), but this was less important than what was happening inside the buildings. In too many of the schools I visited, the concept of teaching and learning that most people would naturally expect to be happening within a school just was not taking place. I saw one class where a teacher stood in front of thirty teenagers virtually reading from a script about the origins of World War II, while his audience chatted to each other – teacher and pupils sharing a room, but studiously ignoring each other – marking time until the bell rang to end their mutual misery. As far as I could see, the school had no goals for the students' learning, or systems in place to make sure teachers were supported to help achieve them.

The leadership and systems which should have been in place to give the pupils a fair chance in life had broken down in many of the schools – or had never been built. It was horrifying and it was eye-opening.

I often get asked why I found the issue so concerning. After all, I wasn't British, was planning to leave the country in a few months' time, and seemingly had had no professional interest or background in education issues. I don't know if I have a good answer for this, but the main thing that struck me at the time was the sheer unfairness. In a wealthy country like Great Britain – one of the first in the world to have universal education and often seen globally as a model to aspire to – it struck me that there was enormous wasted potential here and that this was hugely unnecessary. None of us individually is responsible for this situation, but we can all choose whether we want to be responsible for the solution.

I remember studying slavery in history class as a child and similarly struggling to get my head around it. Slavery violates all of our basic understanding of fairness and human dignity. I kept on pushing my teacher – how could people go along with this? Wasn't it obvious that it was wrong? What sort of society would allow this to happen? He gave a reply that I remember to this day: "Lots of people thought it was wrong, but not enough acted to change it. Who knows what future generations will say about things we think of as normal today?" After seeing the disparities in education in London, I felt that I knew what future generations would say about this issue, and they wouldn't be kind.

With the peculiar openness that comes from being new to a problem, I couldn't help but wonder at what seemed an obvious question: why wasn't there sufficient urgency around this issue? Everyone I spoke to agreed on the scale of the challenge. Everyone agreed on the importance of attracting and supporting additional excellent teachers and leaders into the system to help solve this challenge. Everyone agreed that things had to change. Yet, most also agreed that things probably wouldn't change – even if that had the collateral damage of dooming hundreds of thousands of young people to insufficient life chances.

The more I looked at the situation, the more perplexed I was and the more I began to ask questions – of my colleagues, of people in schools, of business leaders, of friends. Spurred on by the challenge, it seemed to me that this situation could only change if more of those most able to focused their attention on it. There must be a way to attract, support and train Britain's best young leaders to make real substantive change in the lives of these young people. Educational inequality was the biggest social issue in the country. After all, hadn't Tony Blair during the 1997 election listed his new government's three top priorities as "education, education, education"? There was an opening there. It seemed to me to be a rare opportunity to make real, lasting change happen. An opportunity that had to be seized with both hands.

By November at McKinsey, we were finishing up the data-gathering stage of the project and were putting together a thick report in smart white binders. They reminded me of the thick reports in smart white binders that I had helped put together for banks and other clients in previous teams. I sometimes wondered how often those smart white binders were opened after we left and in some cases feared it was infrequently, if ever.

These ones described the issues facing schools in challenging circumstances. Over the past ten years, these schools have had their names changed from "disadvantaged schools" to "schools in challenging circumstances", to "London Challenge schools" – and let's not forget the memorable phrase coined by one ex-minister "schools you wouldn't touch with a barge pole". I've often mused that British education can only be truly considered triumphant when we reach a point where every school in the country can just be called "a school". In nice line graphs and with pages of analysis, the information in our report showed in black and white what tens of thousands of young people and their parents encountered in London schools. Some of the statistics were frightening – for example, children eligible for free school meals earned at least five A*–C GCSE grades at a rate less than half the national average[4].

The partner in charge of the project, Nick Lovegrove,

4. Department for Education, "GCSE attainment by eligibility for Free School Meals", 2002 to 2008.

brought us together in a meeting room and laid the folders out on a desk. We only had a month left but he felt we could take our results further. "Come up with ten ideas for what London businesses could do to change this trend," Nick suggested. "For the three of these you think most likely to succeed, write a more detailed five-page business plan in the next few days. We should include this in our report back to the clients."

While my colleagues developed ideas on how businesses could best help school support functions or building projects, I asked to focus on the area that I thought was most crucial – the leadership gap and how pupils in these schools might gain the classroom, school and system leaders who would help them to succeed at the highest level.

That evening, I sat at my desk with all my meeting notes in front of me, the data from school inspection reports showing what influenced pupil results and all my past reports on how banks might attract the best graduates. I took out a piece of paper and drew a triangle. On the top I put "pupils in challenging circumstances", the ones who needed the better education; in the lower right corner I put "top graduates" the ones who would provide it; and in the lower left I put "businesses and other supporters", the ones who would enable it all. But, what would bind them all together? In the middle I wrote down "teaching" and crossed it out. I tried "support", but that didn't work. I then put "leadership". It was what the pupils needed, what graduates wanted the chance to show and what other organisations could support. It was the missing ingredient. There needed to be a way to create a movement of leaders to help young people realise their potential and access the opportunities that were passing them by.

I worked through the night to finish off a high-level business plan for a charity designed to attract top graduates into teaching. As with most things at McKinsey, this took the form of PowerPoint slides – twenty in total, with another thirty in an appendix. It was all very clear to me how this would work. An independent organisation would need to be created. A CEO hired who could lead it and about a dozen or so employees. It would all be, I thought, fairly straightforward. The charity would get ministerial approval to train teachers in a new way in spring 2002, start recruiting graduates in the autumn, place them the following winter, and start their training the next summer – with 200 great teachers in post for September 2003. These would then serve as the nucleus of a long-term movement of change makers. The £1 million start-up funding required would be raised half from ten private sector donors and half as seed funding from the government.

I made the mistake of showing the plan to my office mates after they woke me up the next morning. At that time, the Muppets figured prominently in our office banter. The four of them often debated back and forth (sometimes with detailed spreadsheets and PowerPoint presentations) on who had been the biggest Muppet that day, the main criteria being the person who said the most idiotic or naive thing. I seemed to win this prize with startling regularity. "It's not easy being green, is it Brett?" laughed one of them, who styled himself after one of the crotchety old men who sat on the balcony pouring scorn on the *Muppet Show* each week. After looking at the plan they decided to name me the Muppet of the Month.

John was a bit gentler. As my manager, he pointed out some difficulties behind the scheme – it wasn't that easy to get laws changed; money was hard to come by; there was not really any clear evidence that top graduates were interested in teaching in these schools (in fact, just the opposite). Training and supporting excellent teachers was not as straightforward as I proposed. Yet, he saw the potential and that this was a useful "thought" paper to include in the recommendations. He would give me the opportunity to present it to our clients – the first high-level client presentation in my career.

I spent days preparing for my presentation – the first time this idea would be explained to an external audience. To me it seemed so obvious – the situation in Britain was fundamentally unfair to many children. This situation could change with the proper leadership from top graduates. Yet, whenever I practised my presentation to colleagues, their looks of scepticism made me feel more and more of a Muppet.

HOW TO WRITE A BUSINESS PLAN

When I started to talk to people about the education charity idea, I kept on getting asked if I had a business plan. At the time, I worried what this meant. Was there some sort of set formula or structure that needed to be followed? What was this mysterious thing called a "business plan"?

I ended up getting hold of a few copies of other business plans that had been used and realised that there was no one common format. Some were as short as a two-page description of an idea, while others were literally hundreds of pages with detailed cost and revenue projections. I took a middle ground. The original business plan for the charity that would become Teach First had six key parts to it that, while they have changed in detail and tone, have broadly served as the blueprint for our work over our first decade.

1. Vision – What are we trying to do? What are our aspirations? For us, it was: "Improve the quality of education for London secondary school pupils in low-income communities by giving them additional dynamic, creative and energised teachers and improve the quality of London secondary schools through long-term active participation of the teachers and rub-off effects among other school teachers and staff." Long term, the plan was to grow the programme to include other low-income areas of the UK.

2. Description of the programme – A who, what and how? This involved a month-to-month plan of what we'd need to do over our first eighteen months, including fundraising, recruiting 200 top graduates, and training and placing them in schools in challenging circumstances. Also, what would we need the various stakeholders to do, including the roles for businesses and other supporters?

3. Competitive Landscape – Who were we competing against? Crucially, I looked to top graduate recruiters in this rather than to other routes into teaching. From the start, I wanted us to be seen as a competitor to Accenture, Civil Service Fast Stream, Deloitte, Goldman Sachs or PwC rather than any teacher training programme currently in existence.

4. Value Proposition – What were the benefits to different stake-holders, including businesses, participants, government and schools? Why should each group be excited about this initiative? For the schools, I wrote down: "We will offer you pre-screened, highly motivated, creative, intelligent and trained teachers to fill your vacant spots. Also, we will continue to support them along the way. This will help solve one of your biggest problems (teacher recruitment), improve the status of teaching in your school, and help improve your pupils' education."

5. Risks – A sensitivity analysis of the effect of different risks and what needed to be done to overcome them. An important section as prospective supporters needed to be able to see that potential problems were being considered and addressed. I actually struggled to fill this out, but got lots of help from people I spoke with! Some of the risks included:

- Difficult to find financial backing for programme
- Government, Teacher Training Agency (TTA – now the Teaching Agency) or schools of education do not support our teachers because of their lack of training
- Headteachers do not want to hire the teachers
- Not enough top university graduates interested in joining the programme
- Participants find they cannot successfully teach in a disadvantaged school environment

6. Appendices – This got into the nitty-gritty and included some detailed information on how the participants would be trained, what a high-level budget would look like, the design of the organisational structure and even the team's job descriptions.

The presentation took place in early December at the offices of London First, off Trafalgar Square in central London. On one side of the table were the clients for our project, including Stephen O'Brien, the then CEO of London First; Julia Cleverdon, the then CEO of Business in the Community; John May, who was in charge of education work at BitC, and Rona Kiley, who was leading on education projects at London First and is the wife of then London Transport Commissioner Bob Kiley. Rona was a native New Yorker with deep interest and experience in the American education reform movement who had recently moved to London due to Bob's appointment.

On the other side of the table I sat with the rest of the team.

John and Nick led the meeting and, after an hour or so, gave me fifteen minutes to present my piece. I took a deep drink of water, began to talk and realised that I was shaking from nervousness. There were sympathetic looks from the other side of the table, which only made me more self-conscious and anxious. Yet, as I got going, my commitment to the concept got me through. Then it came to questions. Someone asked: but how will these people be recruited? I attempted an answer. Someone else asked: how will they be trained? I attempted an answer. Who would run such a thing? I wasn't sure. I could see people exchanging looks. I had run out of time and didn't feel like I had convinced anyone. There was a glazed look in our clients' eyes.

I had seen this look before. In a few previous projects I had spent months working long hours to develop intellectually robust answers to our clients' problems that, in reality, stood next to no chance of implementation

– because there wasn't the willpower and energy needed to push through the challenging recommendations we were making. The most painful example of this was when I worked for a bank in Southeast Asia that was close to bankruptcy. We spent two months working seven-day, ninety-hour weeks to develop a difficult restructuring plan that could, potentially, allow the bank to survive if it was implemented immediately. At the client presentation by the partners leading the project, their board gave us a similar glazed look, thanked us profusely and promptly left for month-long holidays. A few weeks later we learned that a relative of a senior government official had bought a controlling interest in the bank. As a result, its problems were solved – through a government cash infusion. The entire project had been for show. I was really scared that this would be a repeat of that experience – and in this case there was no rich cousin to help the challenged schools on their way.

At the end of the presentation, everyone thanked us profusely for our real focus on the problems at hand and how businesses could ameliorate them. We were thanked for our commitment to the project and we were thanked for such a wonderful presentation. There was then a long pause as everyone looked at each other, satisfied with a job well done. His Royal Highness would get his report and maybe this would move things forward in a positive way. But I was worried. My instinct told me that this would be the end of the idea, not the beginning. I cleared my throat. It couldn't end this way. This problem was too important and the idea had too much potential just to be left in neat white binders. This was a moment in time when silence was not golden. Someone needed to commit to this.

Although I was the most junior member of the team, I raised my voice and gave what I thought was a gentle nudge to the proceedings. What, I asked, did our clients think should be done to further explore the ideas that we had discussed when the team broke up in a few weeks time at the end of the year?

Everyone looked at each other, but Rona took the bait. She suggested that she could set up a conversation with her friend, Sue Lehmann, the chair of Teach For America, an American charity which had some elements in common with the business plan. Maybe that could be the source of some ideas on what could be done next. It was a result and meant that there was life in this yet.

Teach For America is a charity focused on eliminating educational inequity in the United States, which was founded by Wendy Kopp, who famously developed the idea in her senior thesis at Princeton University in 1989. Although Teach For America had been around when I was at university, it was still relatively small in the mid-nineties and I hadn't been aware of it. As we spoke to Sue, we learned that in the subsequent years, when I had been in Asia, the charity had grown tremendously and, by 2002, was recruiting about 1600 top graduates a year to teach in low-income schools across America. It was obvious that there were some lessons from their experience that could be useful.

Sue then put us in touch with Wendy and others involved with Teach For America, as well as a number of other educational reformers in the USA. There was an interesting model there and lots to learn from, but there were also elements that I felt didn't translate into the British context. I understood that Teach For America had faced challenges in getting people to understand its ultimate goal of building a force of leaders for educational change, and I felt that a prominent focus on leadership from the start would be the key to unlocking the problem in the UK. I also saw that Teach For America was navigating a charged education reform discussion in the USA that sometimes positioned them as "outsiders" making change. I felt in the UK a strong focus on collaboration would be critical.

Yet, it was enormously encouraging and exciting to see that such a similar programme had started successfully and was already beginning to show that its teachers were having an impact in the classroom and staying engaged in addressing educational disadvantage in the longer-term. Seeing this early progress in America further spurred my belief that the model could work in the UK.

Over the next few weeks, as our time on the project wrapped up, I worked on tying up the loose ends of the business plan, taking in input from focus groups with London headteachers, university students and educational experts. At the same time, John May, Rona and I set out to see if there might be an educationalist out there who would be interested in leading the idea.

We struggled. I still remember a meeting we had with one individual to whom John introduced us. He was well versed in the British education world, had led a school relatively successfully and was looking for "something different". He believed that young people in many low-income schools were not being taught effectively enough. Sensing a kindred spirit, I talked him through the idea and asked him where he thought it could go. He was clear that we could get a few dozen graduates to teach in low-income schools, potentially those who weren't able to get their first choice of jobs. In his vision, it would be slightly different from the normal teacher training route. But as much as he was pushed, he couldn't imagine something that would have a wider focus on leadership and change. We saw this with many of the people who were introduced to the idea. There was a struggle to think outside of the box and really dream big about what could be achieved. I left these conversations feeling a bit depressed and wondering why some of these really smart people didn't "get" what seemed to me to be so obvious.

In a wonderful example of serendipity, a few days later, I received a crucial call out of the blue. Jo Owen, a successful British entrepreneur, leadership guru and author, had been listening to a radio programme about Teach For America and had wondered if an adaptation might work in the UK. He had contacted them and got through to Wendy who put him in touch with me.

Shortly before Christmas, Jo and I met in the lobby of McKinsey's Piccadilly offices. It was the start of what has proven to be a great mentoring relationship.

At the time, I was deeply conflicted about what my next move should be. I knew that after the holidays, I would be put on another consulting project, probably back in Southeast Asia, and my involvement in this idea would come to an end. While I still didn't think I was the right person to lead it, I worried that the idea would die without my involvement. I had started to feel really depressed about the prospects.

Jo amplified my worries. He was keen to help and support but clear that he didn't have the capacity or interest to lead and push this idea with the level of full-time involvement it needed. Within an hour of meeting, he was also quite clear with me that things would not continue if I stopped my involvement. With a carefully calculated display of flattery and manipulation, he looked me in the eye and said, "This idea needs an outsider to make it happen and, like it or not, you are that outsider. You have the passion, you have the interest and you have started to build the right contacts. You have a greater ability to make this happen than you think. Let's meet in the New Year and figure out how *you* will get this started."

I left our meeting on a high but also frightened by the implications of his words. Pumped up with a feeling that I was on the verge of something that could help transform the lives of thousands of young people in the UK, I was brought screeching down to earth that afternoon when I met a senior civil servant from the government Teacher Training Agency. As I outlined the broad idea behind the initiative, she looked at me with a raised eyebrow and started peppering me with legitimate questions for which I was woefully underprepared.

"How would our trainees meet all sixty-three standards necessary for an Newly Qualified Teacher?"

"How would standard 2.3 be handled based on the recent Ofsted findings and the Commission on Teacher Qualification report?"

"Do you understand the requirements placed on accredited providers in England and how do you plan to meet them?"

I gamely tried my best to navigate around the alphabet soup, but she quickly saw through the fakery. I had no idea how to answer any of her questions and they had the desired effect of making me realise how far out of my league I was and how little I knew. As I came home that evening, I thought glumly about my next move. As well as the wider problems of starting such an unlikely initiative, battling a foreign bureaucracy and having to gain a deep knowledge fast of something I knew little about, there were also the more mundane practicalities. If I did give up my career for such a pie in the sky idea, how would I pay for my living expenses with only limited savings and no family income to fall back on? I didn't even know how long my work visa would enable me to stay in the country!

The next week was enormously difficult as I struggled to make what felt like a life-changing decision. I think there are a few occasions in any person's life when there is a clear fork in the road and a single choice will enable two very different futures. I was acutely aware that this was one of those occasions and, as someone who struggles to make firm decisions in the best of times, agonised over what I should do next. I walked the streets of London, trying to get to a clear place, talked to friends and family, spoke with strangers, meditated and made careful lists of pros and cons, which I then crumpled up because they gave me the "wrong" answer.

Logically, my next step was clear. I should continue in my career and see if I could build a successful professional platform in consulting or financial services. I could then volunteer a bit in a charity and gain some experience and skills. There was no way that I had the experience, maturity, local knowledge, subject knowledge, organisational leadership knowledge, temperament or ability to get such an unlikely idea off the ground.

Yet, emotionally, in my heart, it felt as if there was only one route I could take. The more I thought about it, the more I knew that I was actually incredibly fortunate, since it is so rare to have the opportunity to pursue something you are passionate about, much less one which could move the world to a slightly better place. This was my opportunity and I wasn't sure I would have another. I couldn't get the students I saw in my school visits out of my mind. This idea could change their lives, of that I was sure. They deserved better opportunities and this would create them. If I didn't do it, I would regret it for the rest of my life.

Over the years, I have seen many other people have to make similar choices – it is always a difficult moment. The advice I give is that all successful enterprises seem to have one thing in common – someone involved at some point has to take the plunge and make a commitment to try to make it happen against the odds. If no one had ever taken these risks, we would all no doubt still be huddled in caves, eating berries. On the other hand, I often think that there must be so many great initiatives that have never got going because they have been held back by fear of failure when, in reality, failure is only assured by never getting started. I sometimes speak to people who seem to have such great capacity for leadership and it breaks my heart when they are not able to realise their potential. This is often because they have waited so long for every "i" to be dotted and "t" to be crossed that, before they know it, the opportunity has passed them by. Entrepreneurs have to make the commitment to an idea, despite the uncertainty or risks presented, in order to be successful.

The more I thought about it, the more I knew – I didn't really have a choice.

Christmas lunch sealed the deal. Rona invited me to her house with her family and as she was clearing the dessert asked me where I was with my thoughts. I told her that I had decided I would leave my job to move this idea forwards. Seeing herself a bit as a mother figure, she worried how this could affect my future if it wasn't successful. She promised to help me fundraise the start-up funds through her position at London First, so that I wouldn't have to draw down my savings too far to get it started. This gave me a greater peace of mind to focus entirely on the project after the break.

Once I returned in the New Year, I went to speak to Nick Lovegrove who helped me negotiate a six-month unpaid leave of absence from McKinsey, while letting me continue to work from the London office. This proved crucial as I managed to use – and probably abuse – the company's good will and belief in this project over the next half-year, getting free support and advice from dozens of people, including everyone from senior partners, who were experts in organisational design, to the reprographics team, who generously printed my promotional literature for free.

One of my first tasks was to get a bunch of early supporters of the idea, including Jo, Rona, John May, and a number of McKinsey colleagues, together in a room to plan out what we needed to do. This was absolutely crucial as I knew that I did not have the skills or knowledge to move it forwards on my own. I gave everyone a copy of the business plan I had written and by the end of the meeting we came up with three main priorities we needed to achieve in order for us to launch in summer 2002 and have our first teachers in classrooms by September 2003:

1. Raise funding – we believed we needed to raise £1 million in order to launch the organisation and that the best way to do this would be to find ten founding sponsors of £50,000 each to be matched by £500,000 of start-up support from the Department for Education and Skills (now called the Department for Education).

2. Gain political support – we needed the schools minister to change legislation to allow this programme to become an alternative way for new teachers to gain Qualified Teacher Status (a lifetime qualification enabling them to teach in England).

3. Improve the business plan – develop practical methods to deliver it, including the graduate recruitment and selection, marketing, teacher training, school placement and organisational development elements.

We went to work. Rona, as a consummate connector, brought together business leaders and potential funders. John, with his education experience (he had been one of the youngest primary headteachers in England earlier in his career), helped us to think through training models, while Jo provided the "can do" entrepreneurial cheer-leading, as well as strategic support and a distinguished-looking grey-haired business leader with an impeccable accent to bring to meetings when it was necessary. Meanwhile, a team of dozens of assorted McKinsey consultants, including Nat Wei (who was ennobled in 2010 as Lord Wei of Shoreditch to lead David Cameron's Big Society programme), came on board to volunteer in the evenings, at weekends or between projects to provide some of the expert and technical support for the business plan. Somehow, almost by accident, I had put together a committed team who were each in their own way crucial to our success.

During the first few months, it was difficult to get traction. We had meetings with foundation and business leaders who struggled to understand how we would be able to attract and develop people that they were finding difficult to recruit themselves. One senior exec at a national bank dismissed Rona and me at a fundraising pitch: "There's no way we would support something like this. You don't even have proper marketing material for your idea!" That evening some of the McKinsey marketing team who were volunteering on the project helped me to design a brochure that we could use for future meetings and then, since we had no money for printing, the guys in the reprographics room generously ran off some copies without a cost code. We had our first brochure.

Most of our meetings with senior education experts went the way of my Teacher Training Agency induction. There was a widespread scepticism that we would be able to design a training programme for any sort of teachers – much less excellent ones – that would enable them to teach in schools in challenging circumstances after six weeks of a summer school.

One senior stakeholder we met was convinced it wouldn't work, telling us that our training model was flawed and we had no idea what it was like in our target schools. "The pupils there have no self-control. You need years of experience on how to deal with them." Yet, a few days later he called me with a tantalising offer. He had been in discussions with officials at the Department for Education and Skills and felt there might just be a way to get the funding and political support we needed to get this off the ground. The only difference would be that our people would be employed as classroom teaching assistants rather than teachers, which he thought was a more "realistic" option for what we were suggesting. This also fitted with the government's latest push for increased numbers and quality of assistants in the classroom.

I thought about it that afternoon, but quickly realised that this gift was a Trojan Horse, which would ultimately destroy what we were trying to achieve. If leadership was the core of the problem and leadership was the core of the solution, then we needed to attract people with outstanding leadership potential to lead classrooms. This was the most powerful part of the model. The right people would not be interested in joining if they were not able to really lead and, in the end, they would not have the impact that was necessary to change children's life trajectories. To his great surprise, I called him up and turned his proposal down.

As a result of refusing this suggestion, we became stuck with a lack of political support for the idea. There were regular changes at the Department for Education and Skills, with rapid turnover in ministerial briefs, which made it difficult for things to get moving. Yet, we also knew that, with Tony Blair's promised focus on education, there was real interest in reform in the Prime Minister's Policy and Delivery Units, with the head of the Delivery Unit, Michael Barber, a former professor of education, interested in alternative models of training from around the world.

After weeks of trying to get taken seriously by key civil servants in the education ministry, our luck finally started to change when one of our McKinsey volunteers mentioned that he had heard from a friend that the Prime Minister's Policy Unit was looking into experimenting with new models of teacher recruitment and training. I went back to my office and Googled the name of the head of the Policy Unit, "Andrew Adonis", to see if I could find a way to get his email address or phone number. After being rebuffed by the company's porn filter, which told me that "Adonis" was a banned word, I tried "Prime Minister's Policy Unit" and got the phone number for 10 Downing Street. Without thinking, I immediately called the main switchboard asking to be put through to Andrew. His assistant asked if Andrew knew me and dismissively took down my name and number. I expected never to hear from him, and was shocked when, half an hour later, Andrew called me back and requested a meeting. To this day, I think that must have been one of the most successful "cold calls" to Downing Street ever attempted.

He and his colleagues, including Michael Barber, had been thinking of similar schemes and they were interested in the work we were doing. With their support, we soon got connected with the schools minister, Stephen Timms, who agreed to look at our work.

At the same time, Rona successfully leveraged some of

her contacts to secure a bit of early financial support for the concept. Our first donor was Canary Wharf Group, a developer in east London's Isle of Dogs that houses some of the wealthiest multinational banks and corporations in the world. They were intently concerned about low educational achievement in the surrounding borough of Tower Hamlets, which at the time was one of the lowest performing education authorities in the country. We went up to their office on the thirtieth floor of One Canada Square, then the tallest building in Europe, and met with their CEO, George Iacobescu, who seemed to understand the idea immediately and, in his strong Romanian accent, agreed to give us start-up funding of £25,000, "as well as whatever money you need to print more professional brochures – you won't get anywhere with these."

I imagine that this instinct for seeing something that most people miss is what's enabled him to successfully lead the development of the formerly barren Isle of Dogs into one of the financial capitals of the world.

This money enabled us to hire our first employee, Anesta Franklin (now Anesta Broad), who started as a temporary PA to help us schedule meetings, assist with marketing, ensure follow up, and basically do a little bit of everything. She's still working with us ten years later and has taken on just about every role in the organisation during this time. The money was also critical for our credibility. Not only did we have professional brochures, we also had a serious financial backer – and it is always easier to be the second person to jump in the water.

Finally, we had a constructive meeting at the University of London's Institute of Education, where senior academics such as Professor Geoff Whitty saw the potential of what we were trying to do and helped seed ideas to improve the training and support of the teachers on the programme. This, combined with the early backing of the general-secretaries of the two main headteacher unions, John Dunford and David Hart, who saw the help we could give their members in getting additional talent into their schools, gave us more intellectual heft and helped us to be taken more seriously in the education world.

Momentum was building. Many of the people we were speaking to felt inspired by our vision and became interested in providing funding for a pilot at the very least. Still, it was slow going. After weeks of trying, beyond Canary Wharf Group's donation, there was no additional funding secured. It soon became obvious that potential funders were waiting to see if the government would sign up to support us before they would make a financial commitment.

As we came back from the Easter holiday, government support became our main priority. We slowly began to build relations with the schools minister. Yet, at the same time, I still struggled to gain traction in my meetings with some of the civil servants at the Department and the Teacher Training Agency.

Quite rightly, I'm sure, they looked at me as someone with far less expertise than them, who wanted to use government money to experiment on an untried, untested model that they would not be able to control. The fact that this was not conceived by them probably damaged our credibility even more. What we were trying to do was very different from what most of them felt comfortable with – and I'm sure my perceived arrogance in how

I communicated what we hoped to achieve didn't help matters.

One meeting with a group of senior civil servants went particularly badly. I got a call from the head of their department one morning asking if I could come in that afternoon to "answer some questions" about what we were trying to do. I wasn't wearing a suit that day and, casually dressed, went into a room full of a dozen men and women in their forties and fifties sitting around a table looking much more professional than me. I then proceeded to give a PowerPoint presentation on the project in the worst management consulting style. Looking at it now, I can see it was full of jargon, unsubstantiated hypotheses, and the dreaded sin of too much talking and not enough listening. As I went through my tenth slide explaining how "impactful" this programme would be compared to other teacher recruitment and training routes that were using an "outdated paradigm", I was interrupted coldly by one of the people in the room. "Are you aware that I invented one of those outdated paradigms?" I learned my lesson.

Yet, due to support from Downing Street and interest at ministerial level we eventually got a formal meeting for final sign-off with the schools minister in late April 2002. This was going to be our opportunity to move forwards and get things ready for a launch. I had an excited conference call with Rona and John. We agreed to go all out and invite as many business leaders as we could who supported the initiative in order to convince the minister how serious we were. In the end we had half a dozen leaders join us, including George Iacobescu.

But, as we got into the room, it was obvious the mood was not as we would have hoped. On one side of a long table sat the schools minister, next to the CEO of the Teacher Training Agency, Ralph Tabberer; and spread out on either side were various civil servants, including the person I had severely insulted the previous week.

The minister looked glumly at his notes and shook his head. "I'm afraid that this isn't the right time for this sort of project. This is a costly programme that does not address the real problems that face London schools." He got up to leave. "I'm sorry. Maybe in the future something like this might work."

As he left for his next meeting, some of the civil servants took over the conversation, going into grisly detail on why the project wouldn't work. They felt that we would merely be poaching recruits from other teacher training programmes; that our teachers wouldn't be as well trained or supported as by other routes; that schools wouldn't want to be part of the programme; and that the whole scheme would cost way too much. I quickly realised that the cost projections they were using were wildly out of kilter with ours.

There was a deathly silence from our side of the table. Briefly, I tried to make a case for changing the decision, but was stopped short. The decision was final.

We shuffled out into the waiting room. George put his hand on my shoulder. "It was a good try Brett, but it doesn't look like the timing is right." One of the other business leaders laughed. "That's putting it mildly. I think that was one of the worst meetings in my career." Everyone else nodded. Rona mentioned that I should look at getting my job back at McKinsey. I felt like I had been hit by a bus and didn't know what to say, so probably for the first time in months, I fell silent.

Rather than take the tube, I walked the two miles home feeling numb. I had been sure that this would be successful and had never even contemplated a Plan B. I still don't know why I had such confidence in the idea, but it had never even occurred to me that we could fail. Now, however, for the first time I wasn't so sure. I kept on going back to my visit to the west London school. Would there be something else that could help those children? Is the whole problem so difficult that nothing could succeed, or in the end was it just that I hadn't played our cards as well as I needed to? I was angry with myself for not doing a better job at getting the officials onside and realised it was my fault the meeting had been such a failure.

The next day I woke up and wasn't sure what to do. Should I go to the office? Make phone calls? Go to the cinema? This seemed to be the end and I felt paralysed. I decided to give Jo a call. He was the tonic I needed and was unremittingly positive, almost making me wonder if I had dreamed how dreadful the previous day had been. Using lines that must have been poached from those inspirational office posters everyone hates, he boosted me up. "Brett, you need to remember that no is simply a prelude to yes... Every new idea goes through moments like this... We can either look at this like a cliff that we've fallen off, in which case we're dead, or we can look at it like a valley that we need to climb out of. Why don't we look at it like a valley? Maybe a valley of death?" he laughed. "You just have to believe that we can climb out of this and we will.

If there's any time you need to show a commitment to this, Brett, it's now."

I laughed. "Maybe we can move out of this valley to the next hill. Can we call it a hill of happiness?"

He later confided in me that he had spent hours scripting that conversation to give me the boost I needed. It was a good use of his time, as the psychobabble worked and I moved out of my deep despair to focus on what we needed to do to change the decision. We scheduled an emergency strategy meeting with a number of the McKinsey consultants who were supporting us in their spare time and we planned out whom we needed to influence and how in order to climb out of the valley.

The first thing we agreed on was that things were not as bad as they appeared. We had a number of positives on our side. There were some serious educationalists who were willing to back us, including teacher training experts, union leaders and top headteachers. A group of leaders from major businesses and foundations were willing to give backing if we got government approval. There seemed to be positive support from 10 Downing Street and some of our supporters relayed behind-the-scenes conversations which indicated that even the minister who had turned us down really wanted to give it a go if we could gain the confidence of key civil servants and answer his concerns.

When we came to the nub of it, we realised the greatest mistake we had made was in failing to bring the officials with us. We had not made a clear enough case for value for money or that this idea would actually work. I had communicated our goals in a way that lacked humility and respect for the difficult work many of them were already doing to raise educational achievement levels. We had failed to build a coalition with some of the best officials in the Department necessary to go further with this.

We believed that the best next steps were a two-pronged approach, with some of our backers contacting Downing Street to ask them to approach the Department for Education and Skills to give us another look. At the same time, I was to get in touch with Ralph Tabberer, the CEO of the Teacher Training Agency, to see what it would take to change the "no" to a "yes".

HOW TO TURN A "NO" INTO A "YES"

I've spoken to a number of entrepreneurs over the years who have sadly been unable to overcome some of their early hurdles. In almost every instance they've described their problems as a situation outside of their control. At the same time, just about every successful entrepreneur has experienced one or more "valleys of death"and can explain how they managed to own the solution to climb out of the problem. What is the difference between these two groups? In almost every time, it has involved turning a firm "No" into a "Yes". Potentially the greatest challenge in these situations is holding onto your self-belief – never lose your commitment to the idea. The greatest entrepreneurs have 100% belief in their vision, mission and themselves in a way that can sometimes seem obsessive to outsiders. However, the truth is if they don't believe in it, no one else will.

In our situation, part of the challenge was to understand what the real objection was. I didn't believe that the problems were the officials' stated ones – "it's costly" or "it won't work" – since the amount of money and support we were asking for was so small. Instead the problems were unstated – "it's not under our control", "it might embarrass some of the efforts we've already made" or "we don't trust you". The mistake we made was to spend too much time talking and not enough listening. If we had gone back showing PowerPoint presentations of how brilliantly it would work, it would have scared them even more.

So we changed tack and began listening to their concerns; we tweaked the programme so that it would not impact on their existing work; and we liberally used the word "pilot" to calm their worries. We also brought respected leaders to meetings to show that there was more to us than untested entrepreneurship.

Finally, we didn't make the mistake of burning our bridges when we got the "no" at our first meeting. We managed to find ways to keep the door open and live to fight another day.

I wrote an email to Ralph and surprisingly he came back almost immediately to suggest a meeting. When we got together I realised that he was more excited than he had originally let on about what we could bring to the teaching profession. In retrospect, I had not done enough to include him in the coalition we were building during the previous months. He saw the possibility of us attracting a new group of people to teach in low-income schools, a group that they had struggled to recruit. He outlined his vision of who needed to join the teaching profession by drawing a pyramid with two horizontal lines to split it into three sections. "See, on the bottom we have the 'wills'. They will teach no matter what we do and don't need any marketing. We rely on them. Then, in the middle, we have the 'mights'. These are the people that we're trying to get to join the profession. Essentially, our marketing tries to remove the barriers they believe are in their way. The third group on the top is the one we can't reach: the 'won'ts'. This group won't currently go into teaching and I think you might be able to get them." I felt that this was still too narrow a reading of what we could do as it didn't take into account the long-term change aspect of the plan, but was excited by his support. He agreed to help me develop a way forward that would take into account the minister's concerns, while keeping true to the spirit of our proposal.

We quickly turned things around, agreeing that we wanted to attract a different sort of intake than the Teacher Training Agency was focused on. We also agreed to work with them to put out to tender some elements of our teacher training to university schools of education.

I spoke to Ralph a few years later about this period and asked how it had all appeared to him. He confirmed that he had been unimpressed by some parts of our initial pitch but liked the energy and innovation we brought to the table and keenly appreciated the business link-up, because it was something he felt he had never been able to take advantage of. He could also see that ministers and Number 10 needed him to help, not stand in the way.

Generously, he said to me: "But what I loved most of all was that you listened to our concerns about the scheme and came back to us, just as full of energy and ideas, to ask for help. You were interested in the specifics and were willing to adapt. In the face of that kind of honesty and tenacity, it's always difficult to say no. Essentially, it was your personal choice to come back to me and talk. By doing so, you changed overnight from a threat to an opportunity. And I knew then that it would be wrong to ignore you or to put barriers in your way." There were crucial lessons I learned here about the significance of building alliances and listening more than speaking.

The following week, I was scheduled to go back to New Jersey to attend a cousin's bat-mitzvah. A few hours before my flight, I got a call. The minister wanted to see us again, as soon as possible. Turning around on my way to the airport, I cancelled the trip (my cousin still hasn't forgiven me). It was the same long table, the same people sitting across from us and the same group of supporters. But, this time, the mood and results were very different. The minister smiled at us. "I'm really pleased with the changes you made and happy to support this. Let's schedule a date for the launch."

We went downstairs to the Department's waiting room and Rona took out a bottle of champagne that she had stowed in her bag. We drank it out of plastic cups, celebrating our success as a group of schoolchildren on a class trip looked at us in bewilderment. That was the last champagne I had for a while as the hard work and commitment necessary to make this a success had only just begun.

TEN STEPS TO STARTING A NEW ENTERPRISE

1. Believe in your "light-bulb" moment

When I had my "light bulb" moment about how leadership could help schools in challenging circumstances, I truly believed it would actually happen. The first people I showed it to – my office mates – thought it unlikely to work. However I was convinced it would. I ignored the 90% of people who had negative views and just assumed they were wrong – requiring a great deal of self-belief, bloody mindedness, and (some would say) naivety. People come up with great ideas all of the time, but often lose confidence at the first naysayer. My advice is – keep the faith!

2. Develop your idea and write it down

The next step for your idea is to write it down and really think through the various implications of it. Who will benefit? What are the risks? What needs to happen? This should be a living document that is constantly being updated as you learn more and tweak the plan.

3. Take a risk

At the end of the day, many great ideas never become reality because no one takes the risk to get them started. Keep in mind that it is easy to discount the bigger risk of looking back regretfully on paths not taken. *Carpe diem*!

4. Build a team invested in the idea's success

No one person ever really starts or "founds" something. It is always a team effort. The success of any project depends on the strength of that team as the most important "force multiplier". For us, it included our early financial supporters, consultants who volunteered their time and many others. Probably my most important job during the early months was enthusing and investing them in the idea so that they felt ownership of it. Alongside this team, you need one or more people who play the role of "mentor" and "connector". For me, Jo Owen and Rona Kiley among others best played these roles. I needed people to support my own development as well as ensure I was meeting the stakeholders necessary for the idea to have wings.

5. Listen to your stakeholders

Much of the time during those early months was spent listening. The old adage that a person who has two ears and one mouth should spend their time listening and speaking in this ratio holds true. We met with many university students, career guidance experts, business leaders, civil servants, teacher training professionals, headteachers, classroom teachers, other social entrepreneurs and politicians. All of them had something important to say.

6. Ignore half of what you hear – it will destroy your idea

Crucially, we didn't actually act on everything we heard. If we had, Teach First would not now be in existence. This is where leadership comes in. It is important to hold true to the original idea and, if you believe in it, then don't compromise on the core value proposition. I knew that if we became a teaching assistant programme, then we'd lose our central focus on using leadership to address this problem. I also strongly believed that some of the experts we spoke to were incorrect in their assessment and so we did not follow their advice.

7. Incorporate half of what you hear – it will save your idea

On the other hand, there were lots of things we did respond to. The plan I wrote at my desk back in November had changed drastically by the time we launched Teach First in July 2002. Most of these changes came from great expert advice. We improved the model of our training, focused more on the long-term leadership aspect of the programme and designed a more robust graduate recruitment marketing model – all based on feedback. As you can tell, the trickiest bit is to know what input to incorporate and what to ignore. No one said this would be easy!

8. If you don't ask, you won't get

It's amazing how people are willing to help if they are asked nicely. So many wonderful people volunteered their time and energy to support us. Probably the greatest mistake I made during the early days was being too hesitant to ask for what we really needed, including sufficient funding. As the idea's chief sales person, you need to be bold, because if you aren't, no one else will be bold for you. Don't be afraid to ask, the worst that can happen is someone saying "no".

9. Defy the valleys of death

Every radical new initiative that tries to change the status quo has to go through some valleys of death. If it wasn't difficult, someone else would have done it already. The secret is to remember it's a valley and not a cliff and to plan how to climb out. It just makes the view from the hills of happiness even sweeter.

10. Begin the hard work!

There is a children's song about a bear that climbs over a

mountain, looks as far as he can see, and finds another mountain to climb. This continues *ad infinitum*. Sometimes, I think this is a good analogy for a successful start-up. It's important to enjoy every hill of happiness, but also to realise that, if you're serious about your mission, there's an even bigger hill in the distance, which is going to require even greater skills and commitment.

Sophie

Sophie is a sparky nine-year-old full of creativity. She is especially gifted at drawing and weaving and will give these activities her undivided and consistent attention. Unfortunately her academic progress has stalled completely. Other teachers have not asked Sophie to pick up a pencil at all as she would immediately become violent and abusive, hurting herself and other children. Our teacher later learned from an educational psychologist that Sophie was so severely disturbed by the sexual abuse inflicted upon her by her father and uncle that she could not bear to attempt tasks that might result in failure – she would only engage in activities for which she knew she would receive positive feedback.

Sophie's self-perception would only become more negative if she saw her peers making progress while she did not. So our teacher engaged Sophie in numeracy work that appeared to be playing games. At the same time she encouraged Sophie to write, not with a pencil but with a large paintbrush on huge sheets of paper spread over the hall floor. Each week the teacher introduced new maths games and a smaller paintbrush. She instructed all of the staff to praise any sentence, word or even letter that Sophie wrote with her paint. Our teacher devoted lunch-times to playing maths games with Sophie and pointing out the maths concepts she was so successfully mastering. Sophie left the class above the national average in mathematics and at the national average in literacy.

2

"You are the wrong person to lead this."
The Value of Integrity

In advance of starting to recruit graduates that September, there was a slew of things that needed to happen in only a four-month period. An entity had to be incorporated, a board needed to be appointed, a name developed, and most importantly of all a CEO and team hired.

At that time, I was still technically on a leave of absence from McKinsey and scheduled to return a few weeks later, at the end of July. During the preceding months I had given some thought to what my longer-term involvement should be. For the first few months, I believed that the best role I could have would be to help get things started and then turn it over to a more experienced CEO, returning to McKinsey secure in the knowledge that it was on a positive track.

However, whenever I tried to get potential leaders excited about taking on the role, I was always underwhelmed. An armchair psychologist might say that this was because I subconsciously wanted the role for myself, but I don't think that was my mindset at the time. I would have been ecstatic to have found the right leader and to return to my previous role, secure in the knowledge that out start-up would be successful, since at that time I was fairly sure that I was not the right person to do this.

I lacked the knowledge and experience of setting up or running anything. I knew that I could perhaps grow into the leader that the organisation needed – but only if I could be really honest with myself about my shortcomings and listen to others about how I could improve. I needed to model the value of integrity by giving and receiving honest feedback, valuing others and acting responsibly.

In retrospect, I wonder if my lack of knowledge and experience was bizarrely exactly what this new initiative needed. I was convinced that we could change the world because I simply didn't know any better. I wonder now in my late-thirties, with a wife, two children and a mortgage, if I would still take the risks associated with starting Teach First and if I still have the sense of possibility I had back then. I hope so.

My elevation from junior associate on a leave of absence from McKinsey to CEO was, in retrospect, a low-key and not terribly official moment. During the spring of 2002, Jo Owen accompanied me to a meeting at one of the banks where we were trying to gain support. He was my grey-haired, respectable-background "wing man" at the meeting and noticed that the executives kept on looking to him for answers rather than me. In the end, the meeting was a failure and we did not get what we needed.

Afterwards, we debriefed over a coffee and he looked me in the eye.

"How would you describe your role at these meetings, Brett?"

At that point I introduced myself as "a consultant on a leave of absence to try to get this started". He rolled his eyes and pointed out that this immediately reduced my potential impact and made me seem less important in the eyes of the people we were trying to get on board. No one was going to invest in a consultant on a leave of absence.

Instead, he suggested that I introduce myself as Acting CEO and get business cards made to this effect. I hemmed and hawed. Was this allowed? I had never actually been appointed to any position and it didn't seem right just making this up myself. Jo laughed. Who was there to appoint me? It would show more integrity if we really focused on how to get better outcomes from meetings. People would take me more seriously if I had an official title, which would be better for what we were trying to achieve. Besides, he pointed out mischievously, if everyone waited for an official appointment process before they took on a role, half the leaders you know would never have got to where they are.

As a result, I soon became known as Acting CEO; and so when finally we received ministerial approval and sufficient private fundraising to launch I was already in post. As Jo told me sometime later, "Brett, you were a natural. We needed someone with the energy and you were that person. We simply had to get the old farts, including me, to accept this fact. By signing all your emails 'Acting CEO' you were taking a problem away from the busy and important people: they were delighted that a young whippersnapper was doing the hard graft. They might have patronised you, but in truth they depended on you. And eventually, you could drop 'Acting': of course, they had to keep themselves happy by going through a formal appointment process. But it was a formality, no more."

To be honest, that formal appointment process never happened. When the schools minister approved our launch in May 2002, I tried to create one and wrote a note to some of our early supporters dangling the possibility that it was time for me to return to McKinsey and asking what role they expected me to have in the new organisation. I immediately received a slightly panicked call from Rona. "Brett, you are absolutely vital to all of this. We need you to stay involved. This is a great opportunity for you."

I noted, though, that no exact role was defined and no one was actually brave enough to offer me anything. I thought through my options and discussed them with my girlfriend, Nicole. Her answer was clear. She was ready (and would probably have preferred) to move with me to Singapore where my next McKinsey posting was likely to be, but was convinced that there was no way I could leave this. "You'd be miserable if you left things now. There's really only one option." She was right. I could not possibly then make the case for my being the most qualified person to lead this educational charity. And yet no one else was offering to step forward. At the same time, my employers at McKinsey were in touch asking when I was planning to return. I needed to make a firm choice, for my own mental clarity as much as anything. I could no longer operate with a net – for this to work, I needed to take full ownership and control of the decision myself. I believed at the time that this would show the most integrity in this situation. In July 2002, somewhat recklessly and without anyone's permission, I officially resigned from McKinsey for good and appointed myself CEO of the new charity, never bringing up the question of my official appointment again. Over time, I forgot about it and it wasn't until eight years later that I was officially appointed and given an employment contract from our board when a new human resources director wondered why I was the only one of our 100-odd employees at that time who didn't have any sort of contract in the system. I was probably the longest-serving Acting CEO in history!

HOW TO BE APPOINTED CEO WITHOUT ANY QUALIFICATIONS

If there was a checklist for what a new educational initiative like Teach First needed in a chief executive, it would probably have looked something like this: experience in education; senior leadership experience; start-up experience; management experience; strong networks; expertise in teacher training, teacher recruitment, school relationships, government relations and fundraising. As someone who had been turned down for the only leadership or management role I had ever applied for (head lifeguard at Ocean Cove in Long Branch, New Jersey) and had only been in Britain for six months, my CV would not have made it past the first cut.

Yet, my critical insight from this period is that it was a

moment in time when an opening appeared and if I hadn't had the deluded self-confidence that I was the right person, I would have spent the next decade regretting what might have been.

So what do you need to become a CEO with zero qualifications? The key lesson I have learned from the whole experience of running a start-up that is trying to do "impossible" things is that passion and belief in an idea can get you a long way as a relatively inexperienced leader, but that these are not enough. You also need to have the integrity to recognise the many areas in which you are going to need help, and to be truly open to constant learning and feedback. In my case, I was surrounded by all sorts of great allies, mentors and experts – people far too busy and sensible to jump into running a start-up themselves! – who gave me unending amounts of advice and support. And I try never to forget that I could not have got where I am today without them.

As part of our launch, we also had to clarify the pretty basic question of what sort of legal structure this new organisation should have. From the first draft of my business plan, I was clear on what I wanted here. I believed that it needed to be an independent non-profit charity. I felt strongly that it needed a clearly independent focus and needed to be grounded in our own vision and values rather than someone else's. We could only do that if we were our own bosses.

I was worried that if it became a government-affiliated organisation, a quasi-government organisation (QUANGO), or some other hybrid run by another organisation, then it would prove more difficult to raise money from the private sector and our strategy would be too constrained by short-term political desires.

As a result, Jo and I lobbied hard to be incorporated as an independent charity. With Rona's and others' support, we created a strong board made up of business leaders such as George Iacobescu, Jim O'Neill of BRIC fame from Goldman Sachs (who was one of our first individual donors) and McKinsey's Nick Lovegrove, as well as the secretaries-general of the two largest headteachers unions, John Dunford and David Hart. However, this group became an advisory board and we were pushed to become a charity incubated under the ownership of London First and Business in the Community. These two larger charities were represented by a small group of five trustees who were the actual "owners" of Teach First. These included John May, Julia Cleverdon and Rona Kiley in their capacity working for those organisations. Stephen O'Brien, the CEO of London First, and George, as the only independent trustee, became co-chairs.

Next we needed a name. We had tried lots of different names during our gestation – often using Teach London, Lead or Teach For Britain as holding names. All of these were routinely panned by focus groups of students at top universities that my McKinsey colleagues and I held. (None, however, was hated as much as my idea of using the slogan "Join a crusade against poverty!" which received exactly zero votes from the various focus groups where I proposed it.)

It was clear that patriotism was not going to be the largest draw for our intake. Also, I worried that if our name was too close to Teach For America's in the United

States, then there could be brand confusion and we would not have as much strategic or brand independence as we might want.

So, we had a "name the baby" contest. And, as new parents who fight over "Sebastian" or "Tarquin" will know, this is the most vicious battle of all – everyone has an opinion.

Finding the right name is one of the most difficult tasks in setting up any organisation. The problem is that it's a combustible situation where you have a crucial decision which can have repercussions for decades, everyone has an view and it's virtually impossible to know who is right. The various volunteers and supporters who were helping on the project argued endlessly over what name would be best.

In despair, I brought in some marketing experts who promised us that they would cut through our difficulties and find the perfect name. They nodded at our explanations of the project, took copious notes at various focus groups, and went away for a few days. They then came back with their findings. "You are looking for a special group of people," the top man intoned in an authoritative baritone, like Moses on the Mount. "They are overachievers who like to keep their options open. The most important thing is that you do not, under any circumstances, include the word Teach in the name of your organisation. Since you are looking for people who would not normally be teachers, this word will turn them off. Instead, you should choose from…" And, with an unveiling worthy of the Oscars, he uncovered a page that had two names: "Bridge" and "Learning to Lead". Bridge, apparently because this was supposed to be a bridge from university to the "real world" and Learning to Lead because that's what people would do.

I gamely tried these names out, but as can be imagined they both fell pretty flat. It was Rona who came up with the name we settled on. "Well, we're asking people to teach early in their careers. Also, London First is one of our supporting organisations. We could call it 'Teach London First.'" We soon realised that as we had national aspirations it did not make sense to include London in the name and shortened it to just Teach First. Relieved to have a solution, we stuck with it. The name has been well-liked and has worked because it is clear and simple.

Yet, over time, I've realised that names can actually mean less than all the heat they generate during their gestation. A rose is still a rose by any other name. Even eight years later, Gordon Brown as Prime Minister was still introducing us as Teach For Britain in speeches and policy accounts, seemingly convinced that this was our name. I've learned over time that what counts more is the brand behind the name – does this brand have integrity in terms of its vision or values? After a decade in use, "Teach First" no longer means what those two words' define; instead it now is imbued with everything our organisation stands for and most people no longer even recognise the words behind the brand. This has become even more important as we now recruit a number of more experienced participants into our cohorts and most of our teachers remain in their schools far beyond their initial commitment.

Finally, we needed a staff team. I asked the McKinsey volunteers who had been helping me if any of them wanted to join full-time. There were two volunteers – Paul Davies and Nat Wei. Paul signed on to lead our operations and finance for a nine-month contract before going off to start his own enterprise in leadership training, while Nat signed on to help with graduate recruitment and fundraising and stayed with us for the next three years. Anesta continued to work with us, supporting our operations and fund-raising and is still a member of our team ten years later. Meanwhile, Jo Owen offered to support us a few days a week, ostensibly as director of strategy, agreeing to donate his salary back to Teach First. And Wendy Kopp, the head of Teach For America, e-mailed me the CV of one of her best teachers, Nicole Sherrin, who had won their national Teacher of the Year award and was keen to spend a year in England. I hired her on the spot to support our graduate recruitment and schools relations and she quickly flew over to join our motley crew.

This left us with seven vacancies to fill based on the business plan – someone to lead our training programme and six graduate recruiters and selectors to go out on campuses and help us attract and select our new recruits. We put an advertisement in *The Times* and were inundated with applications.

I had never interviewed anyone for a job before and found it difficult – in many ways the most stressful experience so far. Everyone seemed so good and I was still of the mindset that I wanted to bring on board anyone who agreed with the concept and wanted to help. As a result, I spent hours speaking to each candidate Anesta brought in, convinced that everyone I met was someone we desperately needed. The truth was that we didn't know what we were looking for, much less how to look for it and it was only Jo Owen's and John May's support in the interviewing that helped us to put together some semblance of a team.

We were at the point where our ambition was exceeded only by our poverty, both in money and reputation. We needed to do great things on a minimal budget, so we could not hire a seasoned team. Instead, we tried to find employees with great enthusiasm and energy and the integrity to focus on our mission, even if they had less experience and skills. Most of them were straight out of university and had never worked for a company before. Our first twelve employees had an average age in the early twenties and I was the second-oldest member at twenty-eight. We were a great example of the adage that youth can change the world. Examples throughout history consistently show the same lesson – ambition, belief and energy can sometimes accomplish more than money and experience.

Yet, crucially we were also able to leverage both. I shamelessly used our corporate connections to oversell our establishment backing. We used McKinsey's and Citigroup's plush central London offices to interview and recruit our early employees (and participants), which gave us a credibility that other start-ups could not even dream about. People who would not have given us a second thought were suddenly prepared to sign up to join us, because they did not see us as an impoverished start-up, but instead as a chance to be on the ground floor of an incredibly exciting, prestigious and well-supported new movement.

A week after the interviews, on 15 July 2002, we had

the official launch of Teach First with the new London schools minister, Stephen Twigg. Twigg was best known at the time for defeating Michael Portillo in the 1997 election and our launch was his first act in his new ministerial role. The event was hosted by Canary Wharf in its then glittering function space at Cabot Hall (since turned into a new retail mall). The great and the good of the education world sat around small tables as Nat and I desperately struggled to get our laptop to work for the opening video and PowerPoint presentation. In the end, we had to call McKinsey's Mumbai-based IT help desk who told us to find a screwdriver, remove our computer's hard drive, shake it around and then replace it. I would have thought this was a joke, except that it actually worked and only seconds before the official launch, our hard drive was restored.

Then, another hiccup. At the last minute, I was told that it did not make sense for me to be one of the main speakers during the launch and not to give my prepared remarks, since I wasn't of the same stature as the rest of the guests. As a compromise, since I understood the programme better than anyone else, it was suggested that I come up to help answer questions at the end. I meekly agreed, which in retrospect was a mistake. The launch turned into a series of speeches about the problems in education at the time and the importance of good teachers, but lacked the energy and specificity that I would have hoped for. Too many of the audience believed that we were being set up to find teachers to fill in for Australian or South African temporary staff. In the Q&A section at the end I tried to correct many of the misconceptions about the programme but, even so, many of the participants probably left the event more confused than ever about what we were trying to accomplish. It did not feel like history in the making.

Yet, that afternoon, when my girlfriend Nicole and I went out for a drink with the first twelve employees of Teach First, I sat with my pint and looked around, and for the first time in months allowed myself to feel really happy. We had a great team and our future was bright. It would all work out and our greatest difficulties were behind us. Rather than feel like I had to take the load myself and rely on lots of part-time volunteers, we now had a team working full-time and tirelessly to achieve our vision. It would be unlimited what we could achieve! I grabbed my glass and made a toast "To addressing educational disadvantage!" Everyone smiled and clinked glasses. We had got this off the ground and at that moment we naively had no doubt that we would be successful.

We all promptly took a two-week holiday, probably the last two-week period when I truly never checked my e-mail even once, and then started a one-week staff induction at McKinsey's offices that Paul, Nat and I had planned based on consulting "best practices", which had the twin results of both raising staff's expectations of the level of support they would get and helping to get all the new starters aligned on what we were trying to achieve and the level at which we wanted to work.

We then moved to a tiny, temporary office near Aldgate East and commenced planning for the graduate recruitment season. Within a few days I realised that, rather than making my life easier, having a bunch of employees actually involved an awful lot of work. While I saw this as a movement that was going to change the world, most of the team saw this as a job. And they all had different biases and views. Some of them only wanted to recruit from certain universities. Others felt mistreated if they were asked to do something without the training and support which they felt entitled to, and which we were woefully unable to give. At the same time, I responded by ignoring any chain of management and asking people to do whatever immediately came to mind, even if it directly contradicted what I had asked them to do an hour earlier. I knew we needed to move fast to achieve everything that was necessary and had no time for niceties. It led to a chaotic and uncertain cocktail of stress and bitterness.

This came to a head during a three-day employee offsite meeting that I organised during the first week of September in Oxford. Having no idea how to lead a team, beyond what I had read in books or learned through consulting experience, I asked some McKinsey volunteers to organise an intense, strategic offsite that, in retrospect, would have been more suitable for an experienced senior management team of a large conglomerate. While we spent some useful time agreeing common goals and how to communicate them, we also attempted to complete case studies, problem-solving exercises and strategy discussions that were totally unsuitable for our largely inexperienced group and served to just further confuse and bewilder everyone. The second evening at dinner, when a few people ordered beers, I reminded them of the two-hour group exercise that I had scheduled for afterwards and one of them looked at me and said, "I work better after a few" and ordered beers for the whole team. Soon everyone was downing drinks and refusing to do any more work that evening. The next morning, when it was time to leave, the level of grumpiness was at an all-time high. Nicole picked me up and looked around shocked at everyone's drained faces. "Brett, what happened to these people?" It was clear that, only six weeks in, we were not working in a sustainable way and that my first effort to bring people together had not been a complete success.

That first experience still leaves me with a twitch whenever anyone says "away day", but the truth is that even that first away day did help to unite the team behind common goals and messages, a benefit that we didn't appreciate at the time. We left the experience a bit bruised and battered, but started the year on the same page and, when we split up around the country to recruit the first cohort, could largely speak with one voice.

In the years since, I have continued to see the value in these offsites. Even when we had extremely limited resources during the early years I prioritised them, and every year since we have had the entire employee team go away for three days in September and two days in March to focus on our values, goals and strategy as well as bond as a team. One of the changes I've made is not to schedule events after dinner and not to equate activities with output. There's nothing wrong with people just getting a chance to know each other in a new environment to help them work together better during the year ahead.

Sometimes, the insights from an offsite have to be treated with caution, though. After that first away day I tried a number of techniques to bounce back. I felt that the problem was that we weren't being open enough with each other and had to give more constant and honest feedback. As a result, I implemented fortnightly "barometers" where every staff member would give a point score of how positively they were feeling in different areas. Anesta would dutifully go through the scores and, when we all got together to discuss the results, would pass around a graph showing the total points in a steady and consistent decline. I soon asked her to stop including comparative charts with the results as they were too depressing.

HOW TO RUN A GOOD OFFSITE

First of all, prioritise them! There are always reasons why it is too difficult/expensive/unnecessary to bring your team together, but unread e-mails or postponed meetings are less important than having a unified and connected team. What better way to get a sense of energy at the start or mid-point of a year than to get a bunch of people into one room and let them talk to each other – they become events that the whole organisation looks forward to.

Another key purpose of them is to allow the space for you to reflect purposefully together on your work, how to be more effective and how to have a greater impact. For this to happen it is critically important that they are planned carefully.

The first rule is that they need to, by definition, be off site. There is something about getting away from normal surroundings that enables people to act differently. This does not mean they need to be at expensive surroundings. Universities, schools or other campuses work just as well as posh hotels.

Another rule is to ensure they aren't passive experiences. They need to involve employees from across the organisation in the planning and delivery in order to ensure perspectives of all teams are represented. Most of all the offsite should allow everyone to work together – whether it is the newest assistant or the most senior director – and ensure that there are ways for everyone to feed in and feel useful. Minimise the amount of time sitting in a room looking at PowerPoint slides all together!

Offsites also need to articulate a sense of purpose that connects the day to day with the bigger picture. Our most successful offsites are where the objectives have been clear and where any actions signalled during the time away have been genuinely followed up. Staff must have the chance to question and challenge any new plans so that there is genuine openness.

There needs to be time to allow connections to be made. Don't overschedule the event. The more high-performing the organisation, the more people will need to rely on and trust each other. This doesn't come from structured meetings. Mix up the formats – less talking and more doing generally works well. I've found that trust can often be better built by partnering in a ceilidh dance than in a two-hour, highly structured brainstorming session.

Finally, give everyone some space. One of the biggest disasters we had was when we forced people to share bedrooms for both cost savings and "team building" purposes. We completely underestimated the value people put on having some personal space when they are away from home with colleagues for three days. The lack of personal space caused quite a mutiny and the fallout was huge, reducing the impact of the rest of the event.

The problems were multiple. The pressure was more intense than any of us had ever experienced. What we were trying to do in the space of a few months – set up a new organisation, create a world-class training programme, recruit 200 of the best graduates in the country at a time of economic boom – would have been difficult for an experienced group, much less our band of eager amateurs.

Before that autumn, I had never thought through the implications of leading a team or what it meant to be a manager. All I had wanted was for Teach First to be successful. I was quickly realising that, for this to occur, a lot needed to happen very fast. The website needed to be up and running in three weeks, not the three months that was normal. Messages needed to be agreed! University visits planned! Training programmes organised! Funds raised! I spent my days running from meeting to meeting without any overarching plan and my evenings exhausted and often in tears. I suppose that a more experienced leader would have been able to get through this period with less chaos and better systems, but I wonder if they would have had the passion and commitment (and the naivety) necessary to move as quickly to achieve such impossible things. It's easy to make quick decisions and cut through bureaucracy when there's only a dozen of you packed in one room together.

The peaks and troughs – "valleys of death," which rapidly turned into "hills of happiness" – of that first year came in quick succession. A particular low-point was in Nottingham that autumn when a few of us presented at the university to attract graduates. It was not a successful event – there were only eight students there to meet the four of us, and, of the eight, six were there for the free sandwiches and wine, which we could ill afford. Dejected, we headed back to the hotel.

Because we had so little money, I had us share rooms

in bed and breakfasts that were under £40 a night. For the most part, these B&Bs had what could delicately be called "character". In this one, with a man passed out in the lobby, things looked exceedingly dodgy. Nat and I walked into our room and there was a television that didn't work. When I went to the front desk to ask for it to be fixed, the receptionist looked surprised. "Oi. You didn't pay for TV," and promptly went into the room to remove it. Our two female colleagues came up to me with fear in their eyes. "Brett" one of them started, "we just don't feel safe in this place. We should move somewhere else tonight."

At the time, I was so focused on our goal – "recruit graduates" – and our constraints – "not enough money" – that I didn't act as a responsible manager or colleague. What I should have done is to model the value of integrity by listening to their very real concerns and work with them to find solutions.

Instead, I tried to calm their worries by telling them that everything would be fine and this was better than the places I had stayed in in Indonesia. Besides, it was all we could afford. That night, as she was asleep, one of the women on the team had her bedroom door opened by a strange man who thought it was his room. Shrieking, she woke us up. "This is all your fault Brett!" My other colleagues looked at me accusingly. We changed our hotel policy after that.

The next morning I missed my train back to London as I waited on what turned out to be the wrong platform. Enraged, I went back to the café where everyone was having breakfast. "I can't believe that train left from the wrong platform!" I told everyone. The team looked at me strangely and first one of them and then the entire group started to laugh. After first feeling cross, I quickly realised how silly I sounded and joined them. It served as a curiously cathartic moment. My platform comment showed my total self-belief – the total self-belief that any entrepreneur needs in adversity. On the other hand, it also showed complete self-delusion – why would I think that the train was at the wrong platform rather than me?

Yet, these are part of the rollercoasters that many successful start-ups go through. The lows are very low, but luckily the highs are also very high and, although it didn't feel like it at the time, there were many highs looming on the horizon. The Nottingham event was shortly followed by another recruitment event where the room overflowed.

During the first year at Teach First, the work was intense and I had trouble switching off. I took every problem personally and felt the need to ensure that every element of our work was under my control. I had a recurring dream in which there was a parade of hundreds of people crossing a bridge over a deep chasm and I was building the bridge piece by piece one step ahead of the parade. My great fear was that the parade would fall off the cliff before the bridge was completed.

Part of the concern was whether we would be able to recruit the right graduates – something that at that point had never been done before – and whether we would be able to find the right way to train and support them to make a real difference in the lives of the young people we were trying to help.

However, underlying all of this was the need to ensure we had sufficient funding to pay for the programme and the right staff team and partnerships to implement it. In the end, there was lots of support from others, but still I felt that all of this fell to me and was frustrated that I could only change reality so much. Though we were getting good responses on campuses and recruiting a great group for our first intake, money and staffing were constant worries. Our ambition drastically exceeded our means. While I had the commitment to work towards what we were trying to achieve, I had not yet learned the importance of valuing others and seeing the rest of the team as building the bridge with me.

The one area that was not a problem was office space. During our first few months, we were based in a cramped room near Aldgate East, next to a loud and boisterous pub. But when, during one of our meetings, George Iacobescu, the CEO of Canary Wharf Group and at that point our co-chair, asked what he could do to help, I suggested donated office space. He agreed and by February 2003, we were ensconced high-up in One Canada Square. To get to the office, our visitors and staff had to walk past our neighbours, the European headquarters of some of the most successful financial services companies in the world, skirt around some of the most fashionable shops in the city and wait in a gorgeous marble reception filled with beautiful modern art before taking a lift up to the twenty-nineth floor, where the view was a far vista, overlooking most of North London. Once there, visitors would see a list of our supporters, who included such blue-chip names as Citigroup, McKinsey, HSBC and Deloitte, and probably assume that we were rolling in cash.

One headteacher who visited us for a meeting looked

around at our offices and angrily wondered where all our money was coming from when he was based in a mouldy Portakabin. "I can't even afford IKEA furniture for my office," he huffed.

No matter how many times I explained that the space was donated, it didn't help and people saw us as being much better financed than we were. We all walked a little taller and believed that we were in a world-class organisation, but the truth was the cupboards were bare.

During my time developing the original business plan, I had drastically underestimated the amount of money required to run Teach First effectively and recruit, select, train and support almost 200 top graduates. While at first I put together a well-researched, detailed three-year budget in the plan, I made the mistake of showing it to some McKinsey colleagues who specialised in cost-cutting and didn't have a full understanding of the programme. Their off-the-cuff response when looking at it was that they felt that I was budgeting too much money for the initiative. Without sufficiently thinking through the consequences, I took their advice and cavalierly reduced our needs, cut staff numbers, and brought the original budget down by 50% from my original estimates. The process lacked the integrity to give us the sort of robust, accurate budget that we needed.

This was a mistake. Within the first few months, my team and I paid the consequences.

By January 2003, we were low on cash and every month thereafter I worried about paying salaries. On the twentieth of each month I had a reminder pop up on my calendar to look at our bank balances to see if we could afford our payroll or if people's paycheques would bounce – my greatest fear. (Even today, I still keep this pop-up on my calendar to remind myself of those dark days.) During many of those months, we came close and a few times it was only thanks to a last-minute cash infusion that we were able to pay employees on time. This was an intense pressure that I found difficult to shake off or share. It was a constant weight that would not leave my shoulders.

I barely visited a school at all during that first year and often worried about losing touch with the problem we were trying to solve. Instead, I spent much of my time in some of the most gorgeous meeting rooms in the country, with framed prints by old masters, tea served in silk bags, and freshly baked cookies brought in by waiters. I would nervously explain our plans at Teach First – how we were going to recruit the best graduates; how we would help low-income schools and the young people in them; and how we would love whoever we were talking to to provide support such as coaching, internships or, perhaps, some funding. The meetings would go well and people would be very friendly, but by the time I got to the financial ask, we would have run out of time and I would be unsure how best to press the request. On the occasions that I did manage to get a request out and follow it through appropriately, it was usually for less than we needed.

The truth was that I didn't have enough sales experience. With support from Rona Kiley, who was a world-class networker for Teach First, I would schedule meetings with the top businesses in the UK, which were booming with profitability. The meetings would go well, but we would struggle to close the deal and they would often promise to support us in words and actions rather than cash.

As a result, we got dozens of responses back from company CEOs who thought that what we were doing was a great thing. On the positive side, we had a list of blue-chip supporters which impressed graduates and others. On the down side, many of them saw this verbal and moral support as the end of their responsibility and we didn't have a strategy to take advantage of the opportunity and get the financial support we so desperately needed.

"YOU CAN'T CHANGE THE WORLD WITHOUT BALANCING THE BOOKS"

This is one of the great lines from Dame Julia Cleverdon, our current chair, who has seen too many charities collapse because of lack of financial viability. For any new start-up, cash is king and you can only run on great ideas, energy and fumes for so long without the money to support it. The good news is that money is almost magnetically attracted to great ideas; the bad news is that it's a lot of work to get it. A few rules that I've learned:

1. Set bigger fundraising goals than you think you need

When we launched, I communicated overly modest budgets because I didn't want to scare anyone (or myself) with a large amount that needed to be raised. I also wanted to get things moving as soon as possible and didn't want to feel held back by fundraising. It soon became apparent, as most homeowners know, that things usually cost more than you first realise, rather than less. Start-ups can only run on high-octane energy for so long, before people need support and staffing levels need to rise with outputs. I should have been braver and shown more integrity in budgeting as it would have enabled us to make a greater impact earlier on. Also, counter-intuitively, sometimes larger goals are easier to achieve than smaller ones, as psychologically they indicate greater impact. Large donors take you more seriously and sense you are more ambitious, which can be inspiring for them.

2. Don't let potential funders off the hook

We had many supporters in our early years, often too many. As we were incubated in two business networks – London First and Business in the Community – we found it easy to link into their members. However, many of them felt they were already doing enough by being part of these groups and by pledging their moral support for Teach First. We were not clear enough that we couldn't pay employees with moral support – we needed financial support. You should be explicit about your financial need without sounding desperate and have a clear entry point for supporters in return for any recognition they receive. Stick to this, so as not to end up with a big group of "friends" who don't make a real contribution. You have to believe the benefit you are offering is genuinely worth supporting. Of course, in the case of Teach First, I believed it was.

3. Don't underestimate the importance of managing data effectively

Keeping a record of early interactions with potential funders is vital for effective fundraising. Every meeting, both formal and informal, should be recorded in a meaningful way that employees have easy access to as the organisation grows. Everyone should be able to see who you have spoken to and when, so that they can be fully prepared when approaching these people. Early investment in a database or CRM (Customer Relationship Management) system and embedding its day-to-day use across the organisation pays off in the future, and makes relationship management much easier and more efficient.

4. Exude confidence and belief – people invest in the entrepreneur as much as the product

I spent too much time preparing PowerPoint presentations and Excel spread sheets, coming up with convoluted structures and benefits for various financial supporters. At one level, these are necessary, but the truth is no one donates to a cause because they are going to become a "gold" or "silver" sponsor or because a strategy makes sense on a bunch of slides. They donated to Teach First because they believed in us and, at some level, they believed in me. We were most successful in gaining donations when I made the pitch personally and filled it with emotion and belief in our ability to succeed.

5. Find ways to earn income from appropriate activities

Too many start-ups are unable to grow because they cannot scale up their funding with their ambitions. One way to do this is to try to gain revenue from as much of the value you are adding as possible. Being clear about the benefits you are offering organisations working with you, whether it be in employee engagement opportunities, or profile, is helpful. At Teach First we look for schools to contribute towards our running costs by paying a "recruitment fee" for each of our teachers who work in their schools, on the basis that they receive a real benefit.

6. Always have a clear action plan for follow-up

Honestly, this seems so obvious but in the day-to-day pressures of a start-up it's easy to forget. A meeting is not finished until the results from that meeting are followed through. It becomes too easy to get stuck in the merry-go-round of scheduling and going to meetings and then forgetting what you are there for. Have a clear agenda, understand what you want and remember to follow-up right away.

7. Invest to make a return

As we have grown, so has the need for funds and the need for supporters. I have come to realise that it is vital for start-ups to invest fairly early in a fundraising team to stand a chance of long-term sustainability. A pound spent on fundraising will return at least four more and hopefully a lot more than that, enabling us to have a greater impact more quickly and build supporters who will keep us going in the long term.

There was one month in particular when I was convinced that our money would not last to pay-day. We needed an additional £50,000 immediately to make it through the next month. Rather than having the integrity to share this with my staff or trustees, I bottled up the problem and told no one. I hid in our small meeting room making frantic calls. One, to the Garfield Weston Foundation, paid off and we managed to get a cheque from them only a few days before salaries were due, which kept us going for a little while longer. During the first year, it often felt we were close to collapse at any moment and as a result, not only would the young people we were trying to serve suffer, but also all the people working at Teach First who were now depending on me.

Part of the problem was also that I had trouble understanding our financial situation. From the beginning, I had prioritised the programmatic part of Teach First and had expected the operational side – finances, HR and facilities – to take care of itself. When I wrote the original business plan, I had included a finance director on staff, however when I reduced the budget, I axed this role rather than reduce our number of graduate recruiters whom I thought of as being more crucial to our success.

This was a difficult decision and I'm not sure it was the correct one. In retrospect, I should have shown the integrity of standing firm with the original budget that had been well thought through, rather than listen to my consultant colleagues. It would have forced me to have been more ambitious with our fundraising goals and our supporters. We needed *both* the graduate recruiters and the finance director to be successful. Our lack of sufficient operational support heavily damaged the organisation during those early years. For far too long, our annual audits were nail-biting affairs and we had difficulty proving that we were a long-term going concern. Expenses were often not paid on time and we struggled to put in place good internal processes, with invoices going missing and management accounts full of mistakes.

The lack of proper management almost led to disaster. About a year in, I hired a front office administrator/office assistant, with the longest, multi-coloured nails that anyone had ever seen. After a few months she appeared to be taking frequent holiday shopping trips to New York, which seemed odd for someone on her salary. One day, our overstretched head of operations at the time pulled me into our meeting room. "Brett, there's something strange here." He showed me some recent cheques that had been returned from our bank that were made out in her name with our two forged signatures on the bottom. Wanting to give her the benefit of the doubt, I went outside and asked her to come into the room to explain an irregularity we had just found. She said she would be a minute and promptly left the office, never to be seen again. Luckily, the bank refunded the cheques she had forged, though it annoyed me a great deal that they never pressed charges.

As I was trying to balance the books, I was also learning on the job what it meant to manage and lead a team. I took what I had learned as a management consultant and often used the wrong lessons from it. For instance, I created a complicated bonus structure for employees that involved an organisational pot based on how we achieved goals and a personal percentage based on individual achievements. At a time when we had little money anyway, this made no sense, and it probably served more as a disincentive than an incentive for everyone as it took our focus away from the mission and young people that united us all. I remember one time when I was pushing everyone to improve their graduate recruitment and reminded them that their bonuses depended on us achieving our intake targets.

One of the more thoughtful members of the team grabbed me afterwards. "Brett, you must realise that money isn't what is driving us. We are doing this for the children and their future. You more than anyone must always remember to use that to incentivise us and not some bonus scheme."

I've never forgotten those wise words.

The problem was that I struggled to move back and forth between the different roles of a visionary entrepreneurial leader and a day-to-day manager who needed to guide the detailed work of a team with a very different background from mine. Often people would work hard to achieve something they were proud of and all I could see were the flaws in it, believing that it would not allow us to meet the difficult goals we had set for ourselves and, rightly or wrongly, that I could do it better myself. While in some cases setting a high bar was necessary to push things forwards, I struggled to share this information responsibly and with integrity. In our small office, with no privacy, everyone could hear when I complained about someone's work and I rapidly became Public Enemy Number One.

I realised that in order to carry out my role well, I needed an honest assessment of what I was doing wrong and how it could be fixed. To get this feedback, I tried regular 360-degree reviews where the team would give me feedback through Jo Owen, who would collate all the information and then read out the results unedited. The first one was fairly damning: "Brett gives confusing messages. He's developing his skills in professionalism. His time management is poor. He is unaware of how much work people have to do."

And they got steadily worse. One day, in a David Brent moment of imbecility, I decided to try to model the importance of feedback by making my 360-degree review public and asked Jo to give me the results in front of the rest of the staff so that I could respond in real time. I felt that this would help all of us be more open about giving and receiving honest feedback.

It would have made for cringe-worthy television. As the staff sat in a semi-circle in front of me, Jo read out their thoughts "Brett is diabolically bad at managing Teach First... Brett does not motivate staff... He micro-manages and drives me potty... He needs to stop talking to me." One point made was "I don't know what Brett does. What is he up to day to day? I never see him around!" However, probably the low-point of anyone's 360-degree review in any organisation was "My image of Brett is that he is a cancer on what could be a great organisation. Does he realise how much damage he's causing?" I tried to formulate a response while half the team smirked and the other half looked away in discomfort.

However I experienced an even lower valley of death during the last week of July 2003, almost exactly one year after our launch. It was during our first summer institute and I was exhausted and grumpy. Our relationship with our training partners was tense, some of our participants were unhappy with what they had signed up for and I had not had a day off in months. I had moved to Canterbury to be at our training institute with our new teachers and had worked non-stop over the past month trying to put out multiple fires – some real and some imaginary. Rather than focus on the areas I felt I couldn't control, I spent too much time worrying about details that I could, like designing participant T-shirts or planning the right icebreakers to ensure our teachers all got to know each other.

Our employees were similarly stressed and unhappy. Many of them had not realised the extent of the commitment they needed to make that summer and were surprised by the intensity of it. To make matters worse, a teenaged cousin I was close to died suddenly in a tragic accident. I was devastated. The funeral was in Hawaii, thousands of miles away. I couldn't go to pay my respects and felt like I was hurtling into a bottomless pit.

Only hours after I found out about my cousin's death, I received a call from the secretary of our co-chair, Stephen O'Brien. She said that Stephen wished to meet with me that afternoon in London. When I told her that I was in Canterbury and probably not able to make it up in time, she was firm. I needed to get up to London to see him as soon as possible.

When I came into his office, Stephen laid into me hard. He had heard from members of the staff team that they were unhappy with my leadership. He believed that they were losing confidence in me and weren't sure I was up to the role. Things would have to change quickly if I was to keep it.

I left his office in tears and went through a number of stages of response. My first was anger. Who did he think he was? I had seen little of him over the previous months and rather than lend a hand to help us move forward, he was just criticising. Next was disbelief. My staff team respected and loved me! We had just recruited some great graduates onto Teach First and were running a really good training programme. The first year had been more successful than anyone could have thought possible. I quickly got to the next stage – acceptance. His views were certainly based on reality. I needed to change my relationship with the staff team and learn how to be a more effective manager.

I had a series of mentors who helped me along the way in this. In addition to Jo Owen, Bob Kiley, Rona's husband who was head of Transport for London, met me a few times to advise me on leading an organisation. He was clear. "It's easy to lead a successful organisation with the right people under you and almost impossible with the wrong people. Getting and aligning the right people with the right goals has to be your greatest priority as CEO above all else."

He was right. Unfortunately, in the first few years sometimes hired employees too quickly and impulsively without really thinking through what we needed. At one extreme, we had a young woman in her early twenties who we brought on board to help provide administrative support. She became fast friends with the rest of the team and one day told us about her new boyfriend who had got a good deal on iPods, which she sold to the rest of the staff at a discount. The next week, she didn't show up for work and we didn't hear from her again. No one knew what happened to her until a week later when we saw a picture of her on page two of the *London Evening Standard* with her boyfriend holding a gun at a terrified bank clerk, taken by the bank's surveillance camera.

At the same time, I was too reactive. I would spontaneously change people's job descriptions on their request, because I was so fearful of losing people I counted on. For example, one of my most valued members of staff desperately wanted a management role even though that didn't make any sense in our structure so I created a co-management situation where he and another member of the leadership team jointly managed a team of eight individuals. It was a recipe for disaster as the team did not know who to listen to and everyone felt under-appreciated.

For the same reasons, the organisation rapidly went through a period of title inflation. Since we could not pay market salaries, it seemed harmless enough to give people whatever senior titles they requested. However, this soon backfired as junior members of staff whom we called "managers" complained about being managed by others and demanded more autonomy and respect as befitted their grandiose positions. Similarly, other employees felt they needed ever grander titles to show their additional experience above the managers, so we made up more and more levels, until no one knew what their jobs were, and often neither did I.

After a year of these problems, I realised that, in addition to stronger HR processes, we needed to better define a common culture for Teach First, which had to provide the glue that all employees worked towards. It couldn't just come from me, it had to have the organisational integrity to come from everyone. I had to open up and let others take ownership of what Teach First was all about as a solid foundation to build a strong organisation.

Together, we agreed on what Teach First needed to stand for and what we wanted to represent. It was clear from the start that we wanted to change children's lives. Putting this down in writing, where every word counted, was difficult but it was also hugely beneficial.

During one offsite in our second year the then eighteen members of the team sat around a table for the better part of a day, buzzing on coffee and too much junk food, arguing endlessly over the wording of our collective mission. Were we focused on "educational disadvantage" or "social change"? Our first draft was ludicrously long:

> *Teach First is a charitable education-business partnership that transforms exceptional graduates into inspirational teachers, placing them into schools where they are needed most. In the short term, Teach First teachers will raise pupil aspirations and achievements through commitment, innovation and resourcefulness.*
>
> *These teachers will also gain experience, training, and skills that will help them become a new cohort of leaders both inside and outside of education. In the long-term, these leaders will use their experience, networks, and skills to help solve the root causes of poverty and educational disadvantage.*

We quickly realised it was unmanageable – no one remembered it and there was not a common understanding of what it meant.

The team and I continued to work on tightening the statement. We agreed to limit ourselves to under twenty words to ensure that every part was completely necessary and truly understood.

We finally managed to get our guiding principle down to seventeen words. We explained our mission as "To address educational disadvantage by transforming exceptional graduates into inspirational, effective teachers and leaders in all fields." We made memorising and understanding this part of all our new employees' induction. It served as an enormously important unifying statement of intent.

However, as we have grown, the need to provide clarity

of focus for employees and our wider community has grown too. We've become worried that the mission statement's emphasis on "exceptional graduates" as the agent of change (we have always meant this as graduates with great leadership potential) has been misinterpreted by some.

And so recently, in a bid to focus less on our tactics, and more on our overall vision, we have adjusted the mission statement to articulate what we actually mean by "addressing educational disadvantage". It now states our ultimate goal, that "no child's educational success is limited by their socio-economic background".

Knowing what we wanted to do, we then worked together to define how we would do it. We did this by coming up with the values that all of us agreed to live by and narrowed them down to five words: Collaboration, Commitment, Innovation, Excellence and Integrity. Years later, we further refined these and switched "Innovation" for "Leadership", coming up with more detailed definitions for each. These values helped us understand what we were looking for in people working at Teach First and how we wanted to work on a day-to-day basis. On a personal basis, they helped me change my leadership style and open up my way of working.

Over the past ten years, I have consistently been trying to improve my methods of leadership as I've grown from being an unsuccessful chicken deliverer to the CEO of Teach First. Probably most importantly, I have had to change my style. While in the beginning, I was entirely task and project-focused, I have since concentrated much more on the importance of sharing ownership.

I have finally understood what Antoine de Saint-

Exupéry, the author of *The Little Prince*, meant when he said: "If you want to build a ship, don't drum up people to gather wood, divide the work and give orders. Instead, teach them to yearn for the vast and endless sea." This is the most important task of an organisational leader.

HOW TO UNITE A TEAM AROUND VALUES

Over the past decade, I've learned the hard way how important it is for people to be united around what Teach First stands for and our way of working. A team can accomplish so much more if they trust one another and are rowing in unison than if they are pushing against each other. Common values can minimise the politics and infighting that blemish so many organisations.

As we've grown, this has become even more important. While a group of twenty sitting around a table can easily figure out how to work together successfully, hundreds spread across the country need something else to unite them. These are some of the ways we use our five values of Collaboration, Commitment, Excellence, Leadership and Integrity:

1. We worked as an entire staff team to define them clearly, including why we hold them dear, what they mean and even more importantly, what don't they mean. Using case studies and examples, we have tried to give them a living meaning, rather than let them remain just individual words that can be misinterpreted. "Integrity" can be a tough word to use if it's not well defined, so we describe it as "acting responsibly at all times", including "speaking honestly" and "valuing others". Similarly "Collaboration" and "Excellence" could sometimes be in conflict.

How should we deal with these situations? Getting everyone involved allowed us all to feel ownership of the values and meant that they had meaning to the whole organisation.

2. We hire based on values. It doesn't matter if the role is for an experienced senior director or a new coordinator, no one should be looked at by a potential hiring manager until they pass a value-based interview. It doesn't matter how talented or experienced a potential applicant is. If they don't want to work according to our core beliefs, then Teach First is not the right organisation for them.

3. We regularly publicise our values and their importance. Every meeting room is named after a value. We use our values in our internal and external documentation. Every year, employees nominate and vote on teams which best exemplify each value. The winners receive the highly cherished Teach First Values Awards.

4. Appraisals and promotions are oriented around our values. Every six months, each member of staff is appraised by their manager (as part of a wider 360-degree assessment) based on how they've worked according to the values over the past half-year.

While it sounds like this can lead to a cultish echo chamber where everyone has the same outlook, in reality it helps build the opposite sort of culture. Common values enable employees to have a higher degree of freedom in their work and make it easier for people to collaborate towards common goals. Strong shared values allow the management team to have a greater confidence

> that their teams will act spontaneously in the organisation's best interest and reduce over-reliance on processes and policies. When they are articulated well, values can smooth problems associated with growth, drive performance and broadly ensure a happier working environment.

Underlying all of this, I've realised, in particular, the importance of integrity as a key component of leadership. This is a difficult task, but crucial. It is impossible to grow without constantly collecting and acting on honest feedback.

Modelling the value of integrity has enabled me to grow in confidence and reduce the defensiveness that was too much a part of my leadership style in the early days of the organisation. Last year I asked the staff team to provide another 360-degree review of my work. There are still many areas to work on including "he is often late for meetings, which I find rude". A number of colleagues complained that I don't always realise that everything I say is picked up by more junior colleagues (an example was given when I mentioned to someone that I wanted to be with my family rather than attend a Sunday morning event and it was shared widely, damaging everyone's morale). I was, though, most gratified by some feedback that a long-term member of staff shared, "Teach First has grown sensationally over the last ten years, so has Brett. If he (and we) can maintain the same rate of progress, challenge and change, then the sky's the limit."

HOW TO BECOME A 28-YEAR-OLD HEADTEACHER
Max's story

While my own leadership journey is somewhat unique, through Teach First over 4,000 other young people have embarked on their own journey with their own hills of happiness and valleys of death. One of these is Max Haimendorf.

I first remember Max as being a natural leader at our 2003 summer institute – as well as a constant annoyance. He would regularly approach me with suggestions on how things could improve – "Did you really mean to give that message at the morning meeting?" "Couldn't you communicate your placement processes more clearly?" "Why aren't you focusing more on excellent teaching pedagogy?" The problem was, I knew he was right and didn't have any good answers. For his part, he was just showing integrity by trying to help us improve the programme.

While at university reading Biological Sciences, Max found himself on what he describes as the "Oxford conveyor belt" taking him towards a job in the City. However, Max wanted to do something different. He was looking for something that was respectable and respected, something that was credible, something that gave him options, and, crucially, something that made a difference to the world.

Max was placed in Uxbridge High School, a school in a deprived area on the edge of the M25 that was largely failing its children, with less than 17% earning five or more A* – Cs at GCSE. At the time, a new head, Peter Lang, had arrived determined to improve attendance, behaviour and results (he has improved their results to over 61% gaining five or more Cs or above including English and Maths and received an outstanding by Ofsted in 2011).

116

When Max talks about his first six months in his job, it reminds me of the intensity we experienced when trying to get Teach First started.Max was given a timetable full of bottom sets across all year groups – a challenge for the most experienced of teachers.

Fortunately for those children, he had a hunger to make an impact and to become good very quickly. He soon recognised that what happened outside of the classroom was as important as what happened in it and made it his business to know what was happening throughout the school.

Max was made a form tutor after just three months and was Head of Year by the end of his first year. After his second year, he deferred his offer of a consultancy job in the City to do a third year at Uxbridge. The following year, the consultancy was put on hold again while Max came to spend a few months helping with strategy work in the head office. He worked on a variety of projects including looking at how we recruit career changers, setting up Teach On (a Continuing Professional Development programme for our community who stay in teaching) and fundraising.

During this time he also became very involved in a report that our teachers wrote called *Policy First: Lessons from the Front*, which looked at ways that schools in challenging circumstances could improve. It was this work and a subsequent trip to visit Charter schools in Houston, Texas, that consolidated Max's vision for what a great school looks like.

Unlike so many dreamers, though, Max then took the crucial step from theory to practice. He and five other Teach First teachers got together regularly to plan how they could make the vision a reality. Like me, Max came across people who said that his idea wouldn't work. They said that the model he had seen in high-performing Charter schools was all very well and good, but it couldn't be transplanted into the British system. Max disagreed.

He believed that the very ingredients that made those schools successful could work here:

- Smaller schools
- Relentless teachers who would do whatever it took to change the lives of the children in their care
- More learning time
- A clear belief that every child would achieve access to university
- No excuses

Max's valley of death was when he thought that the school model that he and other participants had invested so much in would never happen. But then he was thrown a lifeline. The ARK schools academy chain had been developing a similar model and were looking for the right person to lead a brand new secondary school, called the King Solomon Academy in Westminster. At just twenty-eight, the same age I was when I founded Teach First, he was appointed the headteacher.

Like me, there were those who said he was too inexperienced to take on the role. But also like me, he had a team of people around him who believed in him, supported and guided him. I can't see how anyone who visits his school now could say that he's not exactly the right person for the job.

The school serves the Church Street ward which has the highest rate of child poverty in Westminster. The local challenges of crime and youth disaffection are significant and the area is in the top 5% of most deprived places in the UK.

However, only four years in, the school is an oasis of aspiration and achievement. School inspectors have rated it as "an outstanding and unique 21st century school". On visiting the school, these high aspirations and the support to realise them are evident. Pupils speak confidently with quiet pride about their school, their own work and their hopes for the future. Every pupil at the school takes part in unabridged Shakespeare productions and learns to play a string instrument to orchestra standard. By the end of year 9, pupils have made dramatically more progress in English and Maths than the national average, despite starting with lower prior attainment. The feeling you get when speaking to both pupils and staff is that something special is going on there. It's a feeling one would want for any child – whatever their background.

Max says one of his motivations is from a fear of failure. Fear of failing himself, the people who believe in him, the children whose lives he has promised to change and their parents who have trusted him. His inspiration comes from the "amazing" teachers, both Teach First and non-Teach First, whom he employs and seeing the impact that they have, every day, on the children they teach.

Rupa

Rupa is an eighteen-year-old Bangladeshi girl who came to school in Year 7 knowing almost no English. She worked extremely hard during her time in school, meticulously revising and pushing her teachers to give her more advanced work. As a result of her commitment, she achieved eight A and A* grades in her GCSEs and moved on to sixth form finishing with four As at A-level. She planned on applying to a local metropolitan university and continuing to live with her parents, but our teacher convinced her to also apply to his alma mater college at Oxford. He supported her in her application and, when she was refused an interview, was so furious that he injured his hand punching his wall at home in frustration. He promised himself that he would do everything he could to fight for her. As he pointed out to me "she is so much smarter and more committed than almost everyone I went to university with. It just isn't fair." He convinced his old college to grant her an interview. He then convinced a friend who has a job tutoring wealthy children on how to prepare for Oxbridge interviews, to work with her for free. She succeeded in the interview and got accepted. However, only then did he realise that she had put this application in without telling her father, who was upset and wanted her closer to home. Our teacher helped Rupa convince her father to let her go further afield. But, he also worries about all the further challenges she will have once she takes up her Oxford place.

3

"Top graduates will never teach in those schools"
The Value of Excellence

Observing New England in the middle of the nineteenth century, Henry David Thoreau put it simply, if a bit melancholically; "Most people lead lives of quiet desperation and go to the grave with the song still in them."

He would have recognised this truth for top graduates in early twenty-first-century Britain even as the level of opportunity for them felt virtually unlimited.

The decade that preceded the recession in 2008 may go down in history as one of the greatest eras ever for career opportunity for able graduates. Tens of thousands of jobs were available that paid far beyond previous generations' wildest dreams. From the moment they attended a fresher's fair, and sometimes even years before that, the best students were treated as valuable commodities whom employers were desperate to recruit.

And, perhaps because of societal pressure (or poor

information) they often made their career choices based more on who had the best marketing than on what would truly enable them to sing. The fact is that a few dozen companies in these fields have been very good at hoovering up great graduate talent and ensuring their status as the most prestigious places to work. Getting a job in one of these firms is seen, among young adults used to a lifetime of successfully passing exams from nursery onwards, as simply the next "test" to pass.

However, we believed that our "impossible" task here was more possible than first appeared. We believed that we could create a new kind of prestigious graduate role. By maintaining high standards and a belief that focusing on excellence would attract excellent people, we could change highly ingrained attitudes. After all, very few children dream of becoming bankers, accountants or consultants as they are growing up. Not very many more teenagers say this even when they enter university.

Part of the appeal of any future career is obviously money; but today this is not so much the case as is commonly supposed. Bizarre as it might seem, numerous studies and surveys have shown that, certainly in recent years, salary is not the top consideration for graduates when choosing careers. Known as "Generation Y", those who grew up in the eighties and nineties are much more interested in other attributes of a prospective job, including whether the position will enable them to "sing their song" as self-actualised individuals. It's the reason that the large accounting firms' recruitment brochures devote so many pages to leadership and development opportunities and much less on the day-to-day responsibilities of an audit. This is now one of the central principles understood by big graduate recruiters in the war for talent and one that we have been eager to capitalise on.

HOW TO ATTRACT GENERATION Y

Teach First launched just about the time that the first members of Generation Y (typically referred to as those born between 1982 and 2002) graduated from university. It has been observed that this generation, with broad generalisations, has a distinct set of expectations from their prospective employers that differs from that of their predecessors in Generation X.

As would be expected, the average member of Generation Y has a clear idea of what they want from work. We tried to capitalise on this:

1. Challenge
This is the first generation to have grown up using technology and the internet on a daily basis. As a result, Gen Y are more comfortable with multi-tasking, which means they are quick thinkers and, when motivated, quick workers. Work that is too slow will bore them and they will quickly move onto other opportunities. This was great for us, as the fast pace of classroom teaching in a challenging school is a big draw for many Gen Yers in a way that it wouldn't have been for previous generations. The best teachers are good multi-taskers, happily able to differentiate between up to thirty pupils in a single class.

2. Constant development
They crave instant feedback and are highly motivated and

ambitious, often expecting management positions within a few years of starting a role. They are looking for careers with continual learning, which will respect and value them in the workplace – supporting them to achieve their own professional development. They are especially attracted by organisations that can offer new qualifications, as these add to their self-managed CV's.

This fits with Teach First's focus on how we can develop our intake through our Leadership Development Programme and how we can support our teachers through the two years and beyond. There has been an unexpected benefit for our graduates in that many have been promoted into middle leadership positions by their headteachers within a few years of starting. Also, one of the best things about teaching young people is constant (and brutally honest) instant feedback. Finally, all entrants to Teach First currently gain a PGCE (Post Graduate Certificate in Education) qualification.

3. Pride
This is a generation that wants to know that the work they are doing matters. They have seen their parents work for organisations that ultimately gave up on them, so for Gen Y the ability to make a difference while progressing their own career development is of huge interest. This is a great selling point for us as we are a mission-focused organisation with a vision that deeply resonates with them. They can feel good about the work they are doing and that it matters – every day.

4. Prestige
It is also incredibly important to the average Gen Yer that their friends and peers respect what they are doing, so status and

brand attractiveness are important factors in deciding who to work for, and how long to stay. We understood that building a "prestige" brand was a crucial part of our positioning from our first days on campus. We fought to ensure that our stands at career fairs were next to those of the most prestigious employers and that Teach First would be seen as a "top" employer as soon as possible. Once they joined Teach First, we wanted to ensure that our participants felt part of a group of successful individuals with whom they could build an *esprit de corps*.

5. Flexibility

Gen Y value a high degree of freedom and autonomy not only in the way they carry out their work but also in the way they manage their own CVs. They do not buy into a long hours culture in the way Gen X did, and while high levels of engagement are observed, they will not show a long-term commitment if their current role no longer stretches or develops them. We wanted to ensure that our intake saw classroom teaching as a real leadership role that gave them the flexibility and autonomy to lead their children from day one. Also, our pitch, backed up with evidence that our programme and the skills gained would allow flexible career paths after they had completed their initial two-years in the job (though a majority do end up staying in teaching), helped attract graduates who did not want to make a long-term commitment to any one career.

During my original leave of absence from McKinsey in 2002, after many persistent attempts, I was permitted a coffee with the director of careers services at one of Britain's top universities. Taking the train from London into what appeared to me as a fairytale world of academia,

I stepped into an ancient stone building and waited in the antechamber to be summoned into his office. As I sat there, I noticed bookshelves lined with texts older than the country I was from.

When I was finally allowed in, the meeting was a short one. He was busy and could not see how I fitted into his day. I asked him how many of his university's graduates went on to teach in low-income schools and he laughed dismissively. "We have a number who are going into teaching, but inner city schools are not the normal destination. I would imagine it would only be a handful each year who would end up in those sorts of schools."

"Is there any way to change this?"

"I doubt it. You have to understand that our graduates have a lot of opportunities available to them. I just don't see many students here going to teach in those schools. Nothing is really going to change that." After a few minutes, he cut me short. "Thanks for coming, but I'm afraid I have another meeting."

I left his office feeling furious and vaguely patronised. On the train ride back, I set myself a deceptively simple challenge, which was to prove him wrong – and not just wrong for a few of his graduates, but for a lot of them.

During my original negotiations with the Teacher Training Agency and government officials, I had constantly pushed for higher targets. Most of the civil servants we worked with suggested we start with a small pilot of thirty to fifty teachers in the first round and, no doubt, this would have made more sense. It would have been less risky and made our lives easier in those early days, but I fought strongly for the opportunity to make a bigger splash

– hoping to start at ten times their projections, with 500.

I believed strongly that we needed to start big in order to really change perceptions. A small programme would not prove anything and would ultimately not be able to catalyse change in the way that was needed. I wanted to make sure we could work with as many children as possible.

We ended up agreeing that our target during the first three years would be set at around 200 per year. While not as many as I would have liked, most of our supporters thought it impossibly large. If we were successful, then right out of the gate it would make us one of the hundred largest graduate recruiters in the UK and probably the third largest social sector recruiter behind the NHS and Civil Servant Fast Stream.

I also believed that we needed to build a unique brand, and to do this, the image we put across that first year was crucial. It needed to have an extremely high level of exclusivity of the type that was not at that point the norm in challenging schools. I thought this was important, both to ensure that we were recruiting the right level of leaders who could successfully raise the achievement level of young people in our target schools, but also to ensure that we were positioning ourselves from the start in a league with the most discerning places to work.

To achieve the level of selectivity required to meet such high standards, I believed that we needed over a thousand good quality applications from eligible candidates that first year. It was going to be an enormous challenge.

We knew that to get anywhere near these numbers, we had to change the ten-second conversation final year students have about careers. For instance, at many of our universities, the typical conversation might run as follows:

– "I've got a job at a global bank/global accounting firm/global management consultancy/magic circle law firm."
– "Brilliant; you're so lucky!" *(Subtext – Bastard. I'm so jealous. You are one of life's winners that I want to become.)*
Versus:
– "I am going to teach in a comprehensive school in challenging circumstances"
– "Brilliant; you're so brave!" *(Subtext – What a weirdo. At least you'll have good stories.)*

In order to attract enough of the best talent into these schools, we were convinced that this conversation needed to change to become:

– "I've got into Teach First and I am going to teach in a comprehensive school in challenging circumstances."
– "Brilliant; you're so lucky!" *(Subtext – Bastard, I'm so jealous. You are one of life's winners that I want to become.)*

We knew this was possible. Other countries had already made the change – Finland, Singapore and South Korea are three examples where teaching is perceived through this high-prestige prism. We also strongly believed that changing the life opportunities of young people in challenging schools might just provide the best opportunity for talented people to break out of their quiet desperation – much more so than the other graduate jobs on offer. However, to make this change, we had to completely transform perceptions. Teaching in a school in challenging circumstances couldn't just become slightly more prestigious than it had been in the past – it had to become *the most prestigious and well thought of graduate job out there.*

We had to reach a tipping point, a sociological term that refers to a situation where a previously rare phenomenon (top graduates realising the benefits of being successful teachers in schools in challenging circumstances) becomes rapidly and dramatically more common. This was about radical, not gradual change. We needed to take the brand name "Teach First" from being meaningless to it being on a par in graduates' minds with other meaning-less words such as "Goldman Sachs", "Accenture" or "PricewaterhouseCoopers".

Malcolm Gladwell, in his book *The Tipping Point* which came out about this time, refers to this as a "moment of critical mass" when "ideas and products and messages and behaviors spread like viruses." I had my entire team read this book and got us together for a strategy day to determine how we could become one of those viruses.

But, we were still stuck with some old ways of thinking.

During the weeks after our launch, we were given a "present" by the state-run Teacher Training Agency. They said that their advertising agency, a global brand, would support us *pro bono* as part of their contract with the TTA. As we were on such a tight budget, this seemed an offer impossible to refuse.

However, it was quickly apparent that free services are not always worth having.

Nat Wei, who was leading our marketing team at the time, and I sat down at the first meeting with a bored-looking partner who acted as though she would prefer to have been anywhere but there. She looked at us disdainfully. It was clear that she was doing this as a favour for the TTA and that it would not be a big priority. When we asked if it was possible to get certain advertisements and marketing ready in time for our launch, she shrugged, "It depends on a lot of factors. I mean, how long is a ball of string?" After hearing this confusing reply a few times, I stopped her. "What does that mean exactly?" She rolled her eyes. "It means that you are asking impossible questions. We don't know what's possible until we do the research and really define our limits."

The difference in our energy levels was clear. As the two of us bounced around the room using superlatives, "the most prestigious", "the best graduates", "most exciting", she nodded, glanced at her watch, and concluded the meeting with the ominous phrase: "let's do some focus groups."

The focus groups they ran ended with a short memo advising us of the unusual and "extremely difficult" nature of what we were attempting to do. We were looking for a very specific breed of graduate, an extraordinary sub species that was hiding from other top recruiters. They called this target audience the "Non Conforming High Flyer" who was ambitious, had the ability to be successful, but crucially, was unwilling to conform to their peers' expectations (basically, they were weirdos). It further reinforced the notion that "the main attraction of Teach First for this audience would be that it is likely to enhance their future career prospects before committing to a set career path. While altruism in the form of teaching is an important aspect of the programme, it is not the primary driver." They suggested that we use "The path to your best possible future" as our slogan.

This unfortunate advice led to probably the naffest advertisement in the history of graduate recruitment – a photo of a dorky young man in a suit (an intern at the advertising agency serving as a model) with a big toothy grin sitting cross-legged on a double decker bus with the slogan "Going to the Top? Take a Different Route."

The agency loved it. I hated it. One of our supporters looked at it and wondered if the man was actually going to the top ward at Accident & Emergency since it was obvious he was going to be knocked off the bus the first time it entered a tunnel.

To my intense embarrassment, that advertisement did make it into some early publications that year, but we quickly stopped working with the agency, realising that just because something was "free" it didn't mean it was right for us.

Unfortunately, though, we probably took too many lessons from those early focus groups and I think this tweaked our messages the wrong way throughout our first years. The truth was that we weren't looking for "Non Conforming High Flyers". We were looking for "High Flyers". Similarly, while future career prospects were an important driver, they weren't the primary driver that we should have focused on. Our focus should have been more on our ultimate goal: developing leaders with the ability to change young people's lives. We were doing the same thing that everyone else had been doing – not having sufficient respect for either the motives of top graduates or the ability of the children in our schools.

Having gathered our team for a strategy day, we decided to present Teach First in a completely different way to traditional teaching offerings. Specifically, we had to do three things:

- We had to make an old profession (teaching) seem new, shiny and prestigious
- We had to appeal to the heart
- We had to appeal to the head

We did this by presenting our "value proposition" as a triangle, with "Leadership" in the middle (looking at teaching through a new prism), "Make a difference" on the top (appealing to the heart); "Gain distinctive recognised skills" on the lower left point and "Access the inside track" on the lower right point (appealing to the head). During our presentations and discussions with students that year, we built in messaging around all three of these elements.

HOW TO CREATE A NEW MARKET

It takes a brave company to leapfrog over their consumers and give them something that they don't actually know they want.

132

The road to success is littered with the wrecks of those who have tried but failed to bring customers with them – anyone still using the Femidom, Palm Pilot or Betamax?

We had made the mistake that so many organisations make and which separates great market-changers like Starbucks and Ryanair from the rest.

If Howard Schultz, the CEO of Starbucks, had done focus groups of British consumers in the 1990s, he would have found that very few would have had expectations of a cup of coffee beyond it being "warm" and "brown". Even fewer would have thought that they would ever pay more than £3 for a cup. No doubt, these few respondents would have been called "Wealthy Fools" by marketing agencies at the time who would have believed them to be too small and difficult to market to a core customer base. Instead, Starbucks and other high street coffee houses saw an opening, created a new market and confidently sold a new product (which was based on an old one) to them. They based their strategy on Henry Ford's line, "If I'd asked customers what they wanted, they would have told me, 'A faster horse!'"

Similarly, everyone knew that airline customers were price conscious, but until Michael O'Leary took over at Ryanair, no one took this to the extreme. No doubt focus groups of consumers would have said that comfort, connecting flights and central airports were important to them and would have gagged at paying extra for things like luggage or drinks. Yet by focusing exclusively on price, Ryanair grew from a small local airline into one of Europe's largest. According to Michael O'Leary's biography, Ryanair is less concerned about a market research approach to route selection and instead advocates one based on experimentation. In other words, they believed that their presence alone could create a demand which may not have existed previously.

> This is what we needed to do. We needed to show some leadership, ignore the focus groups and be confident that we could create a new market and grow a demand which may not have existed beforehand. We needed to be brave.

At about the same time, Nat introduced me to a pair of guys who he was convinced "got us". We ended up meeting in a pub with two men only a few years older than us who had started their own agency and looked the exact opposite of the slick but bored advertisting partner we had met with earlier. A bit hairy and unkempt, they were both convinced that we could succeed. "Yes, I can see it," one of them nodded. "You're looking to create a new future, a completely different reality where the best leaders are in inner-city schools. It's all about attracting and exciting the 'best of the best'. All leadership flows from being a successful leader in the classroom... This is going to be brilliant!" Nat and I nodded to each other. We hired them on the spot.

When I told some of my ex-colleagues from McKinsey about this decision, they were incredulous. "Let me get this straight," one ventured. "You are worried every month about running out of money, yet you are going to use a large part of your budget on a bunch of unproven guys who need haircuts, rather than take advantage of free support from an award-winning, internationally recognised agency?"

I had to admit, it did seem an odd decision, but somehow, notwithstanding their apparent lack of experience, these two young guys seemed to get the high standards we were looking for and understand what we meant about excellence.

Our trust in them was returned when they came up with what I still believe was a revolutionary campaign that showed from the start that we were definitely new, shiny and different. We were not your grandparents' teacher training scheme. It used the tag line "Leaders of the Future, Unite!" with a focus on what the world would look like in 2023. Some of it was pretty outrageous – transatlantic bridges, sky cars, and space colonies, but amidst the science fiction overtones was a powerful message – the best leaders in 2023 would all be graduates who had taught in schools in challenging circumstances through Teach First in 2003.

It fitted in with an online viral marketing campaign movie that people forwarded to their friends; beer mat puzzles; and postcards with King William on the stamp. It did shake things up and did get us noticed.

However, in some ways, even this marketing set us up incorrectly – the focus was on the graduates rather than the pupils. This sometimes led to accusations that we were focused on giving top graduates additional career development rather than supporting our primary beneficiaries – young people in low-income schools.

Another point which backed up this concern was that there weren't actually any pictures of young people in any of our campaigns. I brought this up once, but everyone involved in our marketing unanimously agreed with the concept and I could see their point.

"We're trying to attract a new sort of person into the profession."

"Pictures of cute, smiling children make us look too much like other charities or teacher recruitment routes."

"We need to look different and fresh."

So in the end it was a strategic decision to focus on the graduate, even though the child was always in our minds. Maybe this was the right call – it did enable us to attract a new group of individuals to apply – but I wonder in retrospect if something got lost as a result. Certainly in subsequent years, our messaging began to focus much more clearly on the impact that we wanted our teachers to have on the young people and it is now more child-focused than ever. What I've seen over the past decade time and time again is that the best British graduates want to make a difference and genuinely do care about others more than themselves. Graduates' motives are hugely underestimated and they are far less cynical than people believe. In retrospect, we should have trusted more in the excellence of our intake.

With the marketing all set, we scheduled our university "milk round" visits. Normally, the largest graduate recruiters would plan out their schedule as much as a year in advance, but we only had weeks to go before we needed to attract over a thousand good applications for a career that almost none of our potential candidates were currently thinking about.

Simultaneously, we had to build a website from scratch in order to get it up and running in time for our 1 October campus launch. We had a holding page, but knew that the people we were trying to attract would see our website as our front window and if it didn't portray exactly the image we wanted, we were finished. At the same time, some of our more university-connected employees were convinced that we needed to have a website that would allow candidates to apply online rather than on paper, still a somewhat revolutionary concept at that time. We had no idea how we were going to make this happen.

Beyond basic computer literacy, none of us had any IT experience and nearly everyone we spoke to at the time thought we were working to impossible deadlines with goals and standards that were too high.

I purchased a few copies of the book *HTML for Dummies* for the rest of us to share, and off we went. For three weeks in September, a number of us with no computing experience pulled consistent all-nighters to put together a massive website with close to a hundred pages. Anesta, whose previous job experience was in retail fashion, created our fundraising pages while simultaneously trying to buy a house. She had to wait two months before she had time to buy any furniture.

Somehow, we managed to meet our deadline. The website looked great and made it appear to outsiders that we were a well-financed professional organisation. I couldn't help but think of Peter Steiner's famous *New Yorker* cartoon where one dog types on a computer while telling another "On the Internet, nobody knows you're a dog."

We split up the universities between us and set off. For the first month, we worried that we weren't making headway, with few applications and tiny audiences on campus. For many of the main presentations, we followed a strict choreography. The recruiter, who was normally a recent graduate and could best relate to the audience, would open things up. They would be followed by me who would paint the big picture of the new project. Jo Owen or John May would then follow as the "senior business leader" who would assure graduates that this would be a great path for a bright future; and, finally, Nicole Sherrin, the Teach For America alumna, would explain her teaching role and the impact they could make in the classroom. She would often end her presentation by getting the audience to join her in the "maths dance" that she had taught her classes to help them learn the properties of positive and negative integers.

We would then have some cheap, warm wine, "value" range sandwiches and crisps. Half the crowd would melt away, happy to have got some free food in exchange for thirty minutes of their time. The other half would pepper us with questions, such as who would accredit the training or what salary they would be paid, and I would gamely fudge an answer or promise to get back to the questioner while mentally thinking about how far behind we were in knowing what we were doing and that I was not building the bridge fast enough to ensure we were always a step ahead of our participants.

HOW TO GAIN MARKET ACCEPTANCE

Every year, there are 340,000 graduates, who compete for only 30,000 openings in the national or multinational firms that run organised graduate schemes. Of these, only around 18,500 are based in companies that recruit more than a few dozen a year. There are even fewer very large graduate recruiters. Only about twenty-five recruit more than a couple of hundred a year, with only the three largest, PwC, Deloitte and now Teach First, bringing in more than a thousand.

The history of organised graduate recruitment as a field is actually relatively new as, for most of British history, there were few university graduates and most would almost automatically go into commerce or law. The process of companies touring universities to promote their openings and attract larger numbers of the best students only started in the mid-1960s with what became known as "the milk round", named after the tradition of milk being delivered direct to homes and, in this case, jobs being delivered directly to university students

Over the past ten years of attending milk round events on university campuses, I've noticed that the views of students towards Teach First have changed quite radically. I sometimes think that one of the greatest measures of our organisational progress is to gauge the type of questions we receive.

I've thought of these as the "What is this?" "How does it work?" and "How can it improve?" phases.

Phase 1: "What is this?"

During the first few years, Teach First was a new concept on campuses. The students attending our events were in their penultimate or final years and had usually never thought about teaching in a school in challenging circumstances. The main question we'd get would be: "What is Teach First?" As a result, they needed to be taken through some basic concepts in order to change their mind to join us.

To attract the best graduates, we needed to create a passion that they didn't know existed in them. We needed to excite them about the entrepreneurial and leadership aspect of what they were signing up to.

Phase 2: "How does it work?"

By our third year, most of the best final-year students had an idea of who we were, and the questions got steadily more complex as they wanted to glimpse under the hood and really understand what they were joining. "I went to a low-income school. If I get accepted, can I teach there?" "My friend is on Teach First and struggled in her first few months. What sort of mentor training do you now give?" "Explain to me your alumni programme." The simple answers of the first few years wouldn't work any more. We were already part of their potential career plans and they wanted to probe deeper. Rather than look at us like a fresh exciting venture, they had some more thoughtful questions and concerns that they expected us to answer.

Phase 3: "How can it improve?"

More recently, I have found it exciting to see that the questions at recruitment events seem much more concerned about impact. Most university students' impression of employers is formed when they start on campus, or sixth-form at the earliest. As a result, by our fifth anniversary, we were as established a brand at universities as companies that had been around for many generations.

Because of this, they felt that they knew what we were and how we operated (and they could always look on our website or speak to a graduate recruiter if they had any detailed questions), and their questions at events started to focus on the meaning behind Teach First. It's a welcome development. "Why do you think teachers can make such an impact?" "Why do you think so few students at my university came from low-income back-grounds?" "I have a question about an aspect of your alumni work that doesn't resonate with me."

What this says to me is that we have begun to help change the conversation on campuses. The need to close the education-al achievement gap is a given. We are now seen as an important part of the debate rather than as a potentially risky start-up.

In the first year, we built up to a big event that we had scheduled at Oxford in early November. We knew that this would be important for us, and we had a great recruiter focused on the university, a tall, well-built blonde rugby player who oozed charisma. When we hired him, one of our female employees was in awe, "Wow, he's a real Hooray Henry – exactly what we need." I needed someone to translate for me what she meant.

In the week before the presentation, we went from college to college, frantically passing out our "leaders of the future" materials to everyone we could find and blitzing the careers centre. I surreptitiously moved all of our materials from the "education" section of the careers centre where the administrator had put them, into the "finance", "law" and "business" sections with the hope of attracting people focused on those careers – sure that she wouldn't mind.

During the previous weeks on other campuses, there had been only tiny turnouts of twenty to thirty students each, which had looked pathetic in the large rooms that we booked. As a result, I suggested to the team that we book smaller rooms and lay out less chairs so that it felt buzzier.

That evening, we set up in the basement of the Ashmolean Museum and cautiously placed thirty chairs with our sci-fi themed banners in the front and a table of drinks and snacks in the back and waited. About thirty minutes before the event, as we were setting up, a trickle of students started coming in, asking if they were at the right place. Soon, more and more entered and a bunch of us ferried in more chairs as things filled up. This was soon overtaken by a flood as over a hundred great potential applicants squeezed in to a standing-room-only area to hear our presentation. It was soon obvious that none had come for the free drinks. After the presentation, there was real enthusiasm and the sense that, for many of them, this was the opportunity they had been waiting for. A number came up to me to thank me for this idea, with one saying that it was the first time he had been truly excited about something he might do the next year. It felt to all of us like we had gathered some real momentum, with enough wind in our sails to attract an excellent first cohort.

Later that evening, exhausted, but also a bit giddy after weeks of effort, we boarded the train to our next city. Some of the team and I settled into the smoking carriage, which still existed at that point, with cigars and lager, acting like the twenty-something-year-olds we were, just ecstatic that things were finally going our way. We were going to do this and it was going to work. There were great graduates out there with great values. The only reason no one had found them previously was because no one had believed this to be true. Massive talent had been going to waste, but wouldn't any more. We woke up the next morning with huge hang-overs, but happy – ready to conquer the next campus.

Within a few months, we had our thousand good applications.

The next area we needed to concentrate on was figuring out exactly which of this talent was right for us.

To home into what we were looking for, we asked some of the best headteachers in London what they believed their most excellent teachers had in common. We then did similar work with the recruitment departments at some of our largest business sponsors. What was encouraging was how much the two categories overlapped. Both of them looked for leadership, communication skills, self-evaluation, initiative and creativity and the ability to take personal responsibility. Businesses looked a bit more for problem-solving abilities, while the headteachers focused more on knowledge of subject and humility, respect and empathy.

One head underlined this last competency with a cold stare, "We don't want little shits in our school. They need to have the humility to respect their colleagues – as well as the children they are in charge of." I completely agreed.

We added all of these into the mix of what would make a Teach Firster. A year later, when we better understood the difficult conditions our teachers had to work in, we added an eighth competency – resilience.

We then went through the online applications of the first group of candidates and soon realised that, based on what we were looking for, hundreds of them were nowhere near making the cut. The ones who were left were invited to our first assessment centre – held in donated space at McKinsey's Jermyn Street offices. We spent the day putting candidates through their paces and then long hours into the night arguing about who met the Teach First criteria. Potentially the best decision we made that day was to turn down any candidate whom we weren't absolutely sure about, sticking to our high expectations of the talent we were looking to attract. We modelled the value of excellence and set the bar high that day. Luckily, we set it right.

HOW TO SELECT LEADERS

We assess our candidates in similar ways to other large recruiters. In order to fairly and thoroughly go through thousands of applications each year, we use a strict evidence-based assessment structure that is focused on our set of eight competencies and values. The goal of the process is to give candidates as many opportunities as possible to prove to us that they have all the competencies we are looking for at the level that we think is necessary to be a successful classroom leader. If our assessors can find evidence that the candidate has all eight competencies (and we still have vacancies left in their subject) then they get an offer. If we fail to find evidence of all the competencies then we do not accept them onto Teach First.

The eight competencies we currently look for are:

- Humility, Respect and Empathy
- Interaction
- Knowledge
- Leadership
- Planning and Organising

- Problem Solving
- Resilience
- Self-Evaluation

First, candidates fill out an online application. At this stage, they answer a series of questions which give them the opportunity to provide evidence of some of the required competencies. Our assessor looks for applicants to be as specific as possible with examples, clearly identifying achievements in detail.

Our second round brings people in to attend a Teach First assessment centre. In the early years, we endeavoured to hold as many of these assessment centres as possible at prestigious locations – McKinsey's offices; the fiftieth floor of One Canada Square at Canary Wharf, Citigroup and Credit Suisse have all hosted these. We wanted top talent to realise that we were a serious organisation with prestigious friends. Now, though, we host them ourselves at a well-branded interview suite in our offices. While candidates are waiting, they take in Teach First's messaging around educational disadvantage and how we want to catalyse change.

At this stage, candidates go through a series of exercises. First, they sit down for an evidence-based interview. Unlike other types of selection tools, which try to examine candidates' thinking, this process looks for examples in the candidates' history of when they've successfully demonstrated the competencies we look for. Next, they go through a group case study which helps us understand their ability to work with others, ideally while showing a balance of our competencies of "interaction" "resilience" and "humility". Finally, they attempt what, for many, is the scariest part of the day, a mock-teaching lesson – during the early years, we all pretended to be poorly behaved eleven-year-old students who couldn't understand Pythagoras' Theorem. Potentially terrifying for the applicant, but it does seem to work! Underpinning the entire day are opportunities for the candidate to self-evaluate their work.

By the end of the day, four different assessors will have seen the candidate and scored them on different competencies between a zero and a five based on highly developed definitions of what we are looking for. The day is set up so that candidates have at least two opportunities to show each competency. If they have managed to show all eight competencies at level four or above, they will normally get accepted. If they are on the border, then there will be a discussion around whether or not they showed the eight areas we are looking for to our satisfaction. If we have not seen sufficient evidence of each competency, then they will not get an offer.

As every selection process necessarily has errors, what this means is that we try to prioritise Type I errors (turning away qualified candidates) over Type II errors (accepting unqualified candidates). This is crucial for us to keep our focus on only accepting candidates who have proven their level of excellence to us.

These offers are then dependent on strong references, evidence of degree completion at their predicted level, and evidence that they have sufficient academic background to teach the subject they are applying for.

We made sure that we kept our standards high and focused on proven competencies, rather than anything else. As a result, we only took in about 20% of all applicants, and less than half of the applicants from any one university.

Within weeks, the first shocked calls started coming in protesting at our decisions. Rarely from the students, almost always from the parents.

"Can I speak to the person in charge?"

"I'm in charge."

"You're in charge!? Really? Well, I want to know why Johnny wasn't accepted to be a teacher. I'm a teacher and spent weeks convincing him to join your scheme! He wasn't convinced, but I talked him into it. He has a top degree and you'd be lucky to have him! Do you have any idea what sort of shortage of teachers we have here and how lucky those schools would be to have him?"

The fact that it was the parent calling rather than the applicant, also told us that we had made the right call.

That spring, I received a mysterious invitation to the unveiling of the 2002-2003 *Times* Top 100 Graduate Employers held in the opulent surroundings of Somerset House off the Embankment. Considered the gold standard rating for graduate recruiters, it ranks companies' reputation on campuses based on a simple question which is sent out to over 17,000 final-year students at top universities, "Which employer do you think offers the best opportunities for graduates?" For years, the ratings had been pretty static. We were stunned to be invited – it meant that at least some university students had listened to our call and thought teaching in a challenging school through Teach First offered the best opportunity in the country for them. We placed bets in the office on where we had ranked. The responses ranged from "They just invited us out of pity in the hope that we'll place next year" to a somewhat optimistic "somewhere in the mid-eighties" (my vote).

As we sat there in the auditorium, next to representatives from Deloitte and HSBC Bank, the hosts built up the suspense by starting at number 100 and working backwards. They quickly got through the nineties, eighties and seventies and we were not mentioned. I looked at my colleagues in despair – this wasn't going to be our year.

They continued working their way up the list – "Number 65 – Freshfields; Number 64 – Merrill Lynch," and then "A surprise newcomer to the list, the highest ranked charity in the history of *The Times* Top 100 – Teach First at number 63!"

This was a great moment for me. In less than four years, I had gone from being fired for incompetence as a chicken delivery boy in New Jersey to being the youngest CEO of a top 100 graduate employer in the UK.

But it was a triumph for Teach First. Only a few months after launching, without even any proof of concept or anyone actually hired; with an amateurish website and a group of half-baked marketing notions, we had embedded ourselves deeply into the consciousness of Britain's students. This proved to me just how much people were underestimating the idealism of Britain's top young leaders. There was a gap in the market that students were desperate to see filled. It also scared me – so many people believed so much in what we were telling them... what would happen if we couldn't deliver?

In the end, we had 186 great new participants show up at our first summer institute that year. Because we did not compromise on the importance of excellence, it was slightly less than our goal of 200, but the quality of the group was fantastic. They were eager, entrepreneurial leaders and from their first day together gelled like long-lost friends. We had selected wisely. Looking back, I know we chose well when I see what so many of these people have accomplished over the past decade – becoming school leaders; starting and leading powerful charities that help young people in so many different ways; advising secretaries of state on educational issues; rising up the ranks of industry and getting their businesses more engaged in supporting schools in low-income communities; becoming some of the best teachers in the country, and joining the leadership team of Teach First. They were a pioneering group and each of them will always have a special place in my heart. Teach First never would have made it to our second year without their courage to prove the critics wrong. Recruiting them was a major hill of happiness.

Yet, that hill had a steep decline as the success of the first year made me more than a bit too cocky in the second.

The first thing I did was to go back to the Teacher Training Agency, whose permission we needed in order to grow our numbers, to beg to be allowed to break out of our government-imposed limit of 200 graduates a year. I was sure that if we only had more time to plan, we would find it easy to grow while keeping our quality bar. I asked for 400; they agreed to 250.

However, the rest of my team at Teach First had other ideas. Many of them felt like they had run a marathon during that first year and just didn't have the stamina to do it again. They were shattered – demotivated and mismanaged. By the end of the first eighteen months, about half of the staff left the organisation. Some of them weren't the right fit from the start, but most were too exhausted and fed up with the chaos of our start-up experience to want to continue. I have since seen many start-ups face this challenge. As organisations develop, they require different people and different cultures. We had to make the transition to being more professional and less seat-of-the-pants.

As part of this transition, our first director of graduate recruitment decided to leave the organisation. I advertised for her replacement but was underwhelmed with the response – we just didn't have a strong enough reputation yet to attract the best candidates and we weren't the new shiny place any more for the most entrepreneurial people to work.

I interviewed a number of the applicants who I knew in my heart weren't quite right and didn't share our understanding of the high standards that were necessary for the team. I wasn't sure what to do and came close to lowering my standards. I thought about giving an offer to one of them, a senior recruiter at a large corporate, but the more I spoke to her, the more I realised that she didn't seem to understand or agree with the high quality bar we wanted to put on our selection criteria. Bringing her on board would not have fitted with the value of excellence which I was trying to build.

When one of our employees mentioned that he had heard the head of graduate recruitment at Credit Suisse was looking for a new role, I jumped at the chance to pursue things further.

I sat down for a coffee with James Darley, the European head of graduate recruitment at the bank, and he looked me up and down. It was clear that I was not the one doing the interviewing here. He had spent a large chunk of his life leading graduate recruitment at various companies and had been a director at the Association of Graduate

Recruiters (AGR). He was a serious, experienced professional who was an expert in his field, something no one else in our merry band of amateurs could claim. He also would have been our first hire over the age of thirty (just – he was thirty-two). However, luckily, he was also in the midst of a bit of an early mid-life crisis. He had recently taken a career break to travel around the world and when he returned, realised that he was bored with recruiting for industries he didn't feel passionate about. He wanted to focus on a mission and thought that Teach First might be it.

I told him about the problems we were having that year and he quickly diagnosed the solution – systems, processes, strategies – all of which were sorely lacking. I asked him if he thought we could grow to 250 graduates a year, a number that seemed a Mount Everest to us at that time. He looked me in the eye, "I don't see any reason why you can't be the largest recruiter of top graduates in the country and get thousands of the best coming in. You're not even close to any limit. This is exactly the sort of thing Britain's best graduates are looking for – they just don't know it yet."

I hired him on the spot.

Unfortunately, James came in too late to stop the decline in the numbers for our second year and we dropped to less than a thousand applications, many of them nowhere near the level of graduate that we were looking for. The energy level of that first year had pretty much dissipated and, even if we were not completely in a valley of death, we were at least in a meadow of despair. I had to go back to the Teacher Training Agency cap in hand to apologise for failing to meet our targets, which was embarrassing, especially as they had already earmarked funds to train the phantom spots we had failed to deliver. The official I met with was supportive, but confused. If we had received over 900 applications, then why were we struggling to recruit 250? Couldn't we just take a quarter of the applicants? After all, this was much more selective than any other route into teaching and it seemed a huge waste to be turning away such great people from top universities.

I understood where he was coming from, but stuck to my guns. There was no way I was going to allow anyone onto Teach First who didn't meet our competency bar. Keeping to a strict standard of excellence was too important to our success. I was sure that if some of our participants looked around at a summer institute and felt there were people there who didn't quite fit what they expected, or if some of our headteachers believed that we weren't recruiting according to high enough standards, we would lose our credibility and their support. It would start a downward spiral that would end up destroying the charity. Most importantly, the young people we wanted to help would not have the excellent leaders they deserved in front of them. We needed to keep the bar high regardless of short-term challenges.

It was one of the most disappointing meetings of the year, because I felt that it was my failure of leadership that was preventing us from helping as many young people as we should. I hadn't been building the bridge fast enough to avoid people falling into the ravine.

Yet, a year on, when we were invited back to the *Times* Top 100, we had somehow risen to forty-first. Even though our applications were not showing it, there was a growing number of students at top universities who believed that we had created something special. It was mentioned during the ceremony that, not only were we the highest ranked charity, but we were one of only two organisations in the top fifty that had been wholly founded in the last quarter century (the other was Microsoft). This was definitely something to build on to get us out of our start-up slump.

James set about methodically building his graduate recruitment "machine" and by our third year, even though we had a slight further decline in numbers, we had begun to turn things around, making a base for future growth. From our fourth year (when we recruited 265 new teachers) onto our tenth, we set a steady pace of over 25% growth a year, almost unprecedented in the graduate recruitment field for such a sustained period.

We changed our marketing to concentrate more on "brand heroes" and the idea of what impact they could make in the classroom – focusing more and more on what we wanted them to accomplish and the amazing leadership role they could have with their students.

HOW TO BE A CROSS-DRESSER
Sanju's story

Although about two-thirds of our teachers continue to work in education beyond their original two-year commitment, it is always interesting to me to see how comfortable our community is in, to use Dame Julia's words, "cross-dressing" between different fields and sectors. This has resulted in some becoming leaders in a number of fields working to ensure no child's educational success is limited by their socio-economic background.

One example of this is Sanju Pal, from one of our early cohorts, who worked as a maths teacher at Mulberry School for Girls, a girls' school in Tower Hamlets where 96% of pupils are of Bangladeshi heritage. She was part of a transformation led by a new headteacher, Vanessa Ogden, that has raised the percentage gaining five A* – Cs (including English and Maths) at GCSE from 39% in 2005 to 79% in 2011 and the percentage of students going onto university to 86%. In 2007, Mulberry students represented an incredible 30% of all Bangladeshi girls in England passing A-levels.

Sanju, of Indian Bengali heritage herself, took over a bottom set Year 10 class, who were failing maths across the board and extremely disaffected. She was shocked that many of them could not add simple numbers, operating ten years behind where they should have been in mathematics. For years, they had just been seen as too hard to motivate, with too much emotional instability and behaviour problems to get them over the line. As Sanju said, "It's so much easier to assume that if they are at the bottom of the pile, they will remain there." It was her most difficult class, but also her most rewarding. She worked with them for two years, serving as a role model and slowly building a level of trust and patience piece by piece so that by the end of the second year, though the entire class had been predicted "U" in their Maths GCSE, almost all of the class passed and one girl managed to make close to ten years of progress in the two years and earn a "C" grade.

Sanju had always planned to embark on a career in business

and, after completing her two years, received an offer to join Accenture, where she is a management consultant.

However, her time at Mulberry had ignited a fire within her. Through Teach First, she had met a number of successful entrepreneurs and, with support from her Teach First coach, developed a plan for a new social enterprise called RISE (Rural India School Enterprise) a charity which aims to address educational disadvantage in rural West Bengal, India and to promote social enterprise and global citizenship in students in Teach First partner schools the UK.

It runs three interconnected activities:

- "Yearn to Learn" – A Bengali literacy intervention programme for 10-year-old students who are at risk of dropping out of school in rural West Bengal.
- "Enterprise Challenge" – A unique after-school project that connects students in the UK and rural India through a programme of social enterprise workshops and activity.
- "Survival Week" – An exciting fundraising challenge for students in the UK to be sponsored to go without an item they think is an "essential" – for a week.

Before starting at Accenture, Sanju spent six months volunteering full-time to get RISE going. Since starting as a consultant in 2009, she has continued to grow the charity during her weekends, evenings and holidays. As she puts it, "If you feel passionate about something you make it happen. It's about time management, being organised and managing deadlines." They expect to work with over a dozen Teach First partner schools in 2012 and hundreds of children in the UK and rural India.

In addition, Sanju is also a key member of the Accenture

Teach First network set up in 2009 to raise awareness among Accenture employees about educational disadvantage and to organise programmes and events which benefit pupils in local schools. An example of the key activities run by Teach Firsters working at Accenture is the "Skills to Succeed Accenture Business Class" programme through which Accenture employees work with various schools to deliver interview skills and team-building workshops.

For Sanju her time on the Teach First programme was a life-changing experience: "It's amazing the transformation you go through during those two years in your outlook and your personal development. None of RISE would have happened without that experience."

Late on the evening of 15 March 2005, I was half-asleep, reading in bed, when my mobile went off. It was a blocked number. Intrigued, I answered it. The conversation went something like this:

"Hello."

"Is this Brett Wigdortz?"

"Yes?"

"I have some news to share with you about the Chancellor's Budget Speech tomorrow, but before I do, you have to understand that this is subject to the Official Secrets Act."

"Huh?" Half-asleep, I assumed it was a prank call.

"You cannot share anything I am going to tell you – it's all governed by the Official Secrets Act. Do you understand?"

"Uh, OK..."

"We understand that you want to grow Teach First, is this true?"

"Uh, sure, we'd love to grow."

"Would you be excited about growing from London to four more cities in the next two years and more than doubling in size?"

I sat up, a bit less sure if it was a prank.

"Sure, I'd love to do that."

"Well, listen Brett, your life is about to change. In his Budget Speech tomorrow the Chancellor will announce this expansion. Your dream will come true. Just remember that you can't tell anyone until the announcement."

"No one?"

"No one. And, one other thing, even though we know the name of your programme is Teach First, for some reason Gordon prefers the name "Teach For Britain", so that's the name he'll use in his speech, but don't worry, we'll all know what he means."

"Teach For Britain? Wait a minute..."

"Also, he's going to announce this as being new, even though we all know you've been around for a few years now. Just go with it."

"What?"

And the official hung up.

The next day, not sure if it was a dream or not, I got to our office and turned on the BBC, settling down to watch the entire Budget Speech for the first time in my life. About three-quarters of the way through, I had an almost out-of-body experience, as I heard the Chancellor of the Exchequer, Gordon Brown, say in his ponderous Scottish tones "and I can announce a new 'Teach For

Britain' scheme – extending the Teach First programme, which offers outstanding graduates incentives to teach in the most challenging schools. From London now and Manchester next year, Teach First will be extended to four more cities, starting with Liverpool and Birmingham... I am convinced that Britain cannot afford to waste the ability of any young person, discard the future of any teenager, or leave untapped the talents of any adult."

I let out a whoop of delight in the office, which startled the rest of the staff. This was real and going to change things. I started to think about how many more schools we could work with!

Unfortunately, in the fastest transition from a hill of happiness to a valley of death in my career, our office phones started to ring off the hooks. In the next five minutes I received a dozen calls simultaneously, including from most of my trustees, that brought me down to earth. The first one I answered was from one of my co-chairs. "Brett. What exactly did you agree? Did you check on any of this with your board?" The rest of the board was equally livid and not excited to hear about this growth first on national television. Most of my staff also felt betrayed – angry at the idea that I had promised something without consulting any of them. We were struggling to even stand still: how were we going to accomplish this nationally broadcast goal? What did it all mean?

To be honest, I didn't know. Surprisingly, neither did anyone else.

At a time when I was counting pennies in order to pay salaries, when we were finding it difficult to attract enough of the right standard of candidates to apply, and when my employee team was largely disaffected and rapidly turning over, this announcement was undoubtedly a shot in the arm. Whether it was a shot of adrenaline or arsenic, I couldn't be sure.

When I contacted the Treasury, they had moved onto other things and said that this was an education department issue and that I would have to deal with the officials there to follow through on the Chancellor's announcement.

I went to meet officials at the Department for Education and Skills, who did not have many answers. Not only were they confused about what the announcement meant, they were annoyed at what they saw as a usurpation of their authority. "Well," said one official in a huff. "There's no money in the budget for this, so you'll have to figure out how to meet this request yourself! I'm afraid that we can't help you."

Sure that I had cooked this up in order to grow quicker, they were angry that I hadn't told them in advance that I was working with the Treasury. If only I was so politically astute as to have had such a clever a strategy!

Actually, in retrospect, I think we stumbled into the maelstrom that was the Blair-Brown war of the last decade. I've now seen a few examples where, in the midst of such Olympian battles, petty mortals, even those such as Teach First who have the support of the Gods, are at risk of being destroyed in the cross-fire.

Meanwhile, some of our supporters started to contact us to congratulate us on the Budget announcement and clarify that, since we were getting such a big slug of government money, we obviously wouldn't be needing their financial support any more. It became more and more difficult for me to explain to them just how desperate we were for their funds and how close I was to making redundancies.

Finally, I got a call from an education department official, assuring me that everything had been "sorted out". She was clear: "We now understand the Chancellor's announcement more. Teach First is now legally obliged to double in size in each of the next two years and to grow to four new cities. There's no additional money in the budget for this, but at least you are now clear about what you need to do."

Our mention had been sandwiched between a number of other multi-billion-pound items in the Budget Speech, and yet this official was adamant that there was absolutely no funding for us included in there.

In addition to the financial problems, James looked into the recruitment situation and came back to me with bad news. He believed that growth on this scale and at this speed just wasn't possible. The machine needed more time to ramp up and the only way we would be able to keep to our assessment centre competency bar would be to work towards a more gradual expansion. I knew that James was just as ambitious as I was, so I had to take his warnings seriously.

We could either keep to our value of excellence or focus solely on growth. In my heart of hearts, I knew what the right answer was.

I went back to the officials and told them that, unfortunately, we couldn't do what they asked as it didn't fit with our strategy and we didn't feel confident we had sufficient resources or ability to grow at that speed.

This was followed by one of the most bizarre meetings

I have ever attended, with officials telling me that it wasn't our choice. We had to do what the Chancellor asked, since it had been announced in the Budget Speech. One ominously suggested that, if we refused to comply, the department would have to create a government-run "Teach For Britain" scheme that would compete with us in order to fulfil the promises made – an idea that would waste taxpayer and donors' money, confuse campus and school audiences and lack our values-driven approach.

Luckily, reason prevailed (with the support of some officials and ministers, including Andrew Adonis, who had recently moved from Downing Street and been ennobled into a position as junior minister in the department). After some negotiations, we agreed on a more sustainable growth pattern that would let us to keep our focus on excellence. This incident proved to me yet again the importance of our being an independent charity rather than a government-run or quasi-government organisation. It was structurally easier for us to take a longer-term strategic view, something which is often difficult for officials concerned about getting re-elected after a parliamentary term.

Even though at the time I felt conflicted – I was negotiating for slower growth, which went against every fibre of my being – in the end I'm sure that it was the right decision. This was the start of what felt to me like our tipping point among university graduates.

About a year later, James came up to me. "Brett, this may be a joke, but I wanted to let you know about an application we recently received." He showed me the name of someone who had been invited to an assessment day. It was Nicky Blair, and the home address on the application was 10 Downing Street, London. Nicky passed the assessment centre and got onto our 2007 cohort.

Not only were we getting high-profile applicants, but we had become an established player in the graduate market.

In the 2011-2012 season, we became one of the largest graduate recruiters in the UK, with 1,000 new participants joining us, selected from over 7,000 applications. In our tenth year, more than 6% of all final year students at the twenty-four "Russell Group" universities applied to Teach First, including more than 10% of all final year students at Oxford and Cambridge.

We have also become a constant presence in the *Times* Top 10 rankings, rising year on year to number four (with only PwC, Deloitte and KPMG above us in the rankings) in 2012. In less than a decade, teaching in a school with a low-income intake has become the most prestigious employment opportunity in the country for top graduates who don't want to become accountants!

One of the lessons I've learned through this journey has been the importance of keeping a high quality bar and how excellence follows excellence. If we had taken the easy way out and reduced our standards, I doubt we would have been able to build the reputation to enable us to get to this stage.

That careers service official I met back when we started? Well, we now recruit more of his graduates than anyone else in the country – more than all of the big banks, consultancies, accounting firms and other establishment brands that have been working with his university for decades.

The idea that British students aren't idealistic has

been discredited. They do not want to live lives of quiet desperation. They want to make a difference. They want to change young people's lives. They are interested in more than themselves and getting as high a salary as possible. These days when they have a real choice about the paths they could take, they are choosing to work in some of the most challenging roles in the country. It is then up to us to support them to be as successful as possible in this crucial leadership position.

Jane

Jane is a sixteen-year-old GCSE student in Greenwich who is bright and capable and a natural leader of her peers. When I visit her school, she proudly takes me on a tour, showing off all the great features of the building. Yet, when our teacher first met her, Jane presented a complicated picture. She always seemed to misbehave just enough to get detention, and yet, at the end of that detention, she would beg our teacher to be allowed to stay longer and do jobs around the school. It was only weeks later that she learned Jane's story. She often did not have anywhere to go and the school was the only area of stability in her life. Her father was in prison and her mother often had violent men over. She shuttled between friends' homes, but the chaos was so ingrained that she was often just forgotten, falling between the cracks. Later still, our teacher learned more of Jane's challenges. At fourteen, Jane was arrested for pimping her twelve-year-old neighbours to local boys. Our teacher, who is one of the few people Jane trusts, tried to get social services involved, but struggled to get Jane the consistency of support that she needed. She ended up supporting Jane to get an A in her History GCSE and then to move into a residential sixth-form college where our teacher now hopes she can be supported through A-levels and then to university.

4

"Training them to teach those children will
be impossible."
The Value of Collaboration

Every step of the way during the first decade of Teach First, whenever we've faced seemingly impossible challenges, we have only overcome them through building partnerships and coalitions of support. It was through working with others that we secured the important political and financial support we needed to launch and it was with and through others that we managed to build a strong employee team and recruit thousands of top graduates.

Nowhere has the value of collaboration proven more important than when it came to supporting our teachers to be really successful in the classroom.

At Teach First we have spent much time pondering the age-old question "What is the essence of great teaching?"

It is a simple question, but one which can also be as perplexing, deep and mystical as the greatest of the Zen Buddhist *koans*, such as "What is the sound of one hand clapping?"

In the twenty-first century, the question of what makes great teaching has still not been answered with any degree of consensus.

We have always come at this with the belief that great teaching is great leadership. A great teacher doesn't just impart information, but is someone who actually leads the young people under their care to a place that they might not think possible. This can mean different things for different students, but at the core, it is based on a concept involving higher academic achievement, aspirations and access to opportunities – what we've ended up calling the "3 As".

WHAT IS GREAT TEACHING?

We believe that starting with the concept of what is great teaching is looking down the wrong end of the telescope. Instead, the starting point should be all about what great learning is. Great teaching should make great learning happen, with the child at the centre.

This is even more important in the low-income communities we are serving where great learning is even more crucial for young people to have the opportunity to achieve, aspire and access the same opportunities as their peers from higher-income communities.

As we have learned more about the needs of our students and the impact of our most effective teachers, we have come to the conclusion that pupils who can access great learning have significantly higher life chances by raising their Achievement, Aspirations and Access to opportunity. The combination of the three As empowers young people with knowledge, skills and motivation that enable them to seek out and achieve the lives they want for themselves. We define them as follows:

Achievement

Achievement is about increasing pupils' academic progress, and also about enabling them to experience success and recognition in school. There are large, measurable gaps in academic achievement between young people from low-income and high-income communities. To use one measure, in 2012, only 35% of children known to be eligible for free school meals gained five or more A* – C grades at GCSE (including English and Maths) compared with 62% of wealthier pupils.[1] Yet, a number of Teach First partner schools have more than closed this gap, with at least eight having over 75% of their pupils achieve this benchmark.

Aspirations

Pupils' aspirations are fundamental to their ability to access education and achieve. What is interesting is that recent research has shown that some of the assumed gaps in the aspirations held by young people from different backgrounds do not really exist. Yet, our students often do not know what they need to do to reach their aspirations and often need to have even higher levels of resilience, confidence and motivation than their better resourced peers in order to be successful. We want our teachers

1. GCSE and Equivalent Attainment by Pupil Characteristics in England, 2010/11, Statistical First Release 03/2012, 9 February 2012.

to work to raise their pupils' aspirations and to remove perceived limitations about what is possible. A recent survey showed that 45% of sixteen to nineteen-year-olds who are eligible for free school meals don't know anyone in a career they would like to work in.[2] Our teachers need to help their pupils think about what they want for themselves, to know that they can get there, and to understand what it takes for them to do so.

Access to opportunities

Without access, pupils cannot benefit from their education, nor from the range of opportunities life has to offer. This is about acknowledging and overcoming the barriers which prevent pupils from accessing learning and other education, employment and training opportunities which should exist for them. In 2012, independent school pupils were over twenty-two times more likely to enter a highly selective university than a state school pupil eligible for free school meals.[3] Great teachers can help their classes understand and overcome the barriers that under-line this outrageous statistic.

Underpinning all of this is our belief that great teaching and learning have an important role to play in bringing about societal change. Research tells us that teachers make a difference. As Dylan Wiliam, Emeritus Professor at the University of London's Institute of Education, writes, "In the classrooms of the best teach-ers, students learn at twice the rate they do in the classrooms of average teachers – they learn in six months what students taught by the average teachers take a year to learn. And in the classrooms of the least effective teachers, the same learning will

2."Social Mobility, Careers Advice and Alumni Networks: A Future First Report Into Revolutionising Careers Advisory Services in the UK", 2011.

3. Sutton Trust, "Responding to the New Landscape for University Access", December 2010.

take two years. Moreover, in the classrooms of the most effective teachers, students from disadvantaged backgrounds learn just as much as those from advantaged backgrounds, and those with behavioural difficulties learn as much as those without."

We believe that if teachers are fundamentally focused on setting and achieving goals to raise the achievement, aspirations and access of young people then great things can happen.

However, raising these "three As" is a hugely ambitious goal, one which has inevitably invited some scepticism in the education world.

In our early days, this scepticism manifested itself in two key areas of concern.

The first was that my pitch might have been slightly off when I enthused about the "exceptional graduates" we were attracting. Most observers heard "posh brainiacs who are going to be eaten alive by more streetwise kids". Partly this was poor communication on my part – after all we were looking to attract people who had leadership skills, not those who only knew how to get good grades. I probably also overdid it a bit on pushing how many great Oxford and Cambridge graduates would be joining us – to the aversion of people who graduated from other great universities.

The worry was that, since many top graduates came from a certain background (though from the beginning our intake has had a very diverse socio-economic background) and the pupils in our schools came from a different background, they would find it difficult to understand and respect each other, much less work well together.

It seemed to be a given among a surprising number of our early contacts (especially middle class business and policy leaders) that young people in the schools we wanted to work with would not listen to teachers who went to highly selective universities and were, therefore, too posh. Further underlying this was that our teachers might even be too posh for the professionals already in the schools and, as a result, the staff room would turn into a battleground of class warfare. It was somehow assumed that the two groups not only used different accents, but spoke completely different languages and were so alien to each other that communication would be nearly impossible.

I would get used to meeting potential supporters in their plush offices who would listen intently to my spiel, nod and express support for the idea that all young people should get an excellent education. They would then lean back, raise a finger, and come back to me with what they would see as the insurmountable objection to Teach First working. "But won't the other teachers and young people in these schools object to having your teachers there?"

The short answer is, "no". This is the dog that has not barked. Like the Sherlock Holmes deduction in the mystery "Silver Blaze", it gives an interesting clue by virtue of not being a significant problem.

In hundreds of schools over many years, I have only rarely seen a situation where pupils or staff in a school with a low-income intake have not worked well as a group together with Teach First teachers. Sure, there are some-times tense individual relationships, especially during our first year in a school when the role of our teachers and how they are being trained is not well understood. There have also been a handful of hires who perhaps should not have made it onto the programme, or who have not been successful in their respective schools. But overall relationships have been incredibly positive. It is unusual for schools that have relevant vacancies not to continue to take more teachers from Teach First after they first partner with us.

I think there are a few reasons for this. We choose our teachers based on competencies which include humility and respect. They join the programme because they want their students to do well. Our training consistently reinforces this and the importance of collaboration in achieving it. We do not believe that great teachers can close their classroom doors and teach in isolation, not least because it prevents any further professional development and improvement. As a result, they normally prioritise working as good colleagues with other professionals in the school. In addition, the idea that our intake comes from a certain economic background is not accurate. A higher proportion of our teachers were eligible for free school meals as young people than the population as a whole. In 2012 24% of our new teachers had been eligible for free school meals or educational maintenance allowances when they were in school. Many went to Teach First schools themselves and managed to be the first generation in their families to move onto good universities, seeing Teach First as a great way to give back and help the next generation to follow them.

Most importantly, though, I believe the reason this

dog has not barked is because it's based on a fundamental misunderstanding of the situation in schools in challenging circumstances. The truth is that in schools across the country young people want to learn and teachers want their schools to be successful. Coming from a family of educators, I have always believed that as long as our teachers are working in partnership to help thestudents do the best that they can, then they will be treated as valued colleagues and classroom leaders. This has turned out to be the reality.

The second concern was to do with how we were going to train and support our teachers – and this one was actually more pressing. I really didn't know.

From my first meeting with the government official who assailed my lack of knowledge on the issue, it was clear that this was my greatest leap of faith. When I suggested to officials or educational experts that our teachers would have a six-week residential as part of their two-year training, they would hear "being thrown in at the deep end with only six weeks of training compared to a normal one-year teaching certificate." Broadly the belief was that many more of these teachers would sink than swim in such circumstances.

Intuitively, I believed that people with strong leadership potential would have the skills to be on their way to being great teachers relatively quickly, but that they would also need a great deal of support and development.

During my original leave of absence, I once spent a few hours brainstorming at a whiteboard with a senior supporter from the University of London Institute of Education and John May, a former primary school headteacher. We mapped out the framework for how such a training programme could look.

It would start with an intense "boot camp" residential summer institute that would include professional pedagogy and subject-specific training as well as classroom experience. This would be followed throughout the first year with classroom observations by trained university tutors as well as regular subject-training days twice a term. Throughout that year, the participants would put together a portfolio of evidence and written assignments which would culminate in them returning to the summer institute to show the university representatives that they met the standards of Qualified Teacher Status. It would be a chopping and changing of other recognised teacher training routes, but would have all of their best elements in a differently organised way.

I fixated on the importance of the summer institute. It would be a key element to bringing people together, building an *esprit de corps*, and setting our new teachers up with the right attitude and skills before they dived into the deep end that autumn.

This fitted in well with new government priorities to open up teacher training. Over the past half-century, the philosophy of what makes a qualified teacher has gone through almost a complete 360-degree change, from the idea that anyone with the right skills could stand in front of young people without any particular training or degree, to the philosophy that held in the later half of the twentieth century that teachers needed a university degree and to go through a clearly academic training programme, usually resulting in a bachelor's degree in education or a one-year post-graduate certificate of full-time academic training.

However, in the years before Teach First, the Blair government, under the intellectual horsepower of Andrew Adonis and Michael Barber, had opened things up, a trend that we were riding. As a result, there were a number of new routes that had already been piloted for experienced professionals to get qualified as teachers, including routes that allowed people to train in schools while working as a teacher. When we stuck our head over the parapet to start Teach First, some of these experiments made our training programme, with its mix of university partners, pedagogical training and a focus on qualifications, seem less radical by comparison. It's always easier to be a second-mover when trying to create radical change.

HOW TO BUILD A WIDE COALITION OF SUPPORT

Another supposedly insurmountable issue that was often mentioned to me was that the British teacher unions would find it difficult to accept Teach First, and that this might potentially serve as a barrier for schools that wanted to participate in the programme. The unions were sometimes portrayed as unreformed Trotskyites who opposed all change. Though I quickly found this to be untrue, it was something that worried me a great deal in the early days. I followed a three-step process in my relationship with the unions as well as other important stakeholders, which has seemed to work over the past decade:

1. Show respect, prepare and listen

Most of my extended family are members of teaching unions in the United States. I came to the relationship with a general respect for the idea that teachers deserve to be supported by a professional body.

We also proactively approached the unions, rather than wait for them to come to us. Before Teach First launched, I asked for meetings with senior officials of the main unions and openly and honestly talked through with them what Teach First was trying to do. I asked them if they had any concerns and listened to what these were. Some of them, such as ensuring our teachers received the correct level of pay and benefits and gained full Qualified Teacher Status through the training, were areas that we were in full agreement on. Others, such as ensuring that the unions could come to the summer institute to meet the new teachers and advertise for membership, also seemed new ways in which we could build positive relationships. Finally, they enabled me to understand concerns around the idea that we might be recruiting academically brilliant graduates who did not have the level of humility or communication skills to lead in a classroom. As a result, we could ensure that we would better publicise exactly what we were looking for and help clarify our communications in advance.

2. Submerge egos

I quickly realised that I was not the right person to lead the meetings with the teacher unions. Like many other professional communities, the UK education policy sector can be hard to penetrate, with its own acronyms, history and social connections. As a young American management consultant with no educational experience, I needed supporters who could represent Teach

First at the meetings and inspire trust. At the first meetings, I was lucky to have David Hart and John Dunford, the general secretaries of the two main headteacher associations, to ensure the teacher unions understood that what we were up to was not as threatening as might first appear.

Later, I brought James Learmonth to the meetings. James was the director of the Centre for Educational Leadership and School Improvement and a well-regarded leader in London education as a former head, inspector and local adviser. He had previously been a member of one of the unions and was friendly with many of their senior executives. He was also deeply committed to the Teach First mission and became a quick supporter and great advocate.

3. Be opportunistic

Timing was crucial. All the planets were in alignment for one lucky moment – our moment. When we were getting started there was a lot going on in the education realm, with all sorts of initiatives being launched by a reforming government – academies, floor targets, new testing and other school requirements. As a result, there were a number of areas of change that the unions were trying to influence that worried them more than Teach First. At the same time, many of their members were supportive of us since, due to existing recruitment issues, they saw the need for additional excellent teachers in London schools.

However, to get started, we needed a training partner. When the education minister approved the launch of Teach First during our meeting in spring 2002, he agreed that the government would fund the training of our teachers at around the same level that they funded other new teachers' training. This would be paid to a university, who would ensure our participants were ready to teach and gained full qualifications.

But the tripartite relationship between us, the Teacher Training Agency (who administered the funding) and a potential university partner was ill-defined from the beginning. One of my non-negotiable points was that the university should feel accountable to us and not just the government. After all, this was the Teach First programme and we needed to be in charge of the messaging, recruitment, training and all elements of the programme. We should choose our university training partners since, in essence, they would be working for us.

Not surprisingly, the officials held a different view. We knew nothing about teacher training while they (as the name of their agency implied) knew everything. They were adamant – we were to have nothing to do with the training. They would select the university training provider through a bidding process that we would be excluded from. They would then tell us who it would be. The training provider would then be in charge of ensuring our people were good teachers and running the training while we would be in charge of finding them and, in the words of one official, "all the leadership, businessy stuff".

In the end, with support from Ralph Tabberer, their CEO, they agreed to fudge the issue, suggesting that we "feed into" the tendering document and then provide one of the three votes on the panel. I agreed. We could be outvoted by the TTA representatives, but at least the universities would see us from the start as one of the organisations they would have to report to.

Getting the tendering document and process right did lead to some tense meetings and petty bureaucratic games. These would normally entail one of my team and I travelling to the TTA's headquarters near Victoria Station. We would be ushered into a conference room and met by seven or eight officials crowded around a boardroom table. Three would take notes, three would nod silently and the remaining two would speak to us in the firm voices that presumably they usually reserved for naughty children they encountered in school. After one meeting, I heard one official snigger to another in a voice too loud to be an accident, "What a Mickey Mouse organisation!"

Tired of being outnumbered and treated with such lack of respect, I once pushed for them to come to our offices for a meeting, which they finally agreed to. I'm ashamed to admit that I dragooned my entire team into our tiny meeting room with the goal of, for once that year, outnumbering the officials in a meeting. Not only were my employees all frustrated with having to waste their time, but it didn't work. The eight of us sat there stewing when the TTA team strolled in with nine officials in tow.

During the preceding month we had already started working informally with one university, who we hoped would end up partnering with us, but the officials were clear that this could destroy the whole tendering process, leading to potential European Union court proceedings where we could be liable. They ordered us to stop all communications with any university representatives in the run up to the tender. In essence, this meant that from September to December 2002, as we were recruiting our first cohort of teachers on campus, we were in purdah, unable to move forwards with any of our training or to begin to plan for the first summer institute that was due to start that coming June. It also meant that we weren't able to "sell" the idea of a Teach First training to any universities or explain the sort of innovative, high-expectations programme we were trying to create. While the graduate recruitment and selection work we had developed was turning out to be fresh and cutting-edge, the development of our training for these people was stuck in a bureaucratic morass.

The tender went out in October and the sealed bids were to be returned the week before Christmas for us to go through and decide our partner. The wait was torturous. However, I had no choice but to cool my heels.

We met at the TTA's offices at midday on the Friday before Christmas, 20 December, 2002. To have some more experienced support, I asked Jo Owen to the meeting to provide back-up and also invited Rona who was going to have to come late. In honour of the festive season, the officials brought out plates of tuna fish sandwiches and M&S Luxury Mince Pies. In front of each seat was an official tender scoring sheet with points from 0 – 10 in six different areas in order to grade the bids at European Union tendering standards.

Next to the scoring sheets was the bid folder. It was thin. We opened it up. There was one bid in there. Jo and I exchanged looks. Not great, but all we needed was one good bid. Hopefully, they would have a good understanding of the programme and what our expectations were.

Unfortunately, they didn't.

As we read through the bid, the panic in the room started to rise. They wrote that they could train up to 100 people that year (we were recruiting 200). They suggested much of the training could be achieved through watching video lectures since few of their professors would be available to work that summer (we wanted a residential course). They believed that the teachers could be supported and trained to lead a class by the middle of their first year (we had promised our intake they would start teaching in September). Either they had lost their nerve or we were asking for an impossible feat.

The top official in the room pulled out her scoring sheet. "Well, let's get going, then." Jo and I looked at each other. There was no point. The bid didn't meet any of our needs. Jo asked if we really needed to go through the scoring as it was obvious that it did not have a suitable standard. Everyone around the table glumly agreed. We had 200 top graduates joining us in six months, but no training partner or clear way forwards.

As we sat there, utterly dejected, Rona walked in with a party bag full of pieces of chocolate cake for everyone and carrying balloons from London First's Christmas party lunch, which she had left early. "How is everyone?" she asked in a bubbly voice. "Am I too late? Have we already picked our partner?"

We had hit another valley of death.

During the week between Christmas and New Year, as most of Britain shut down for the holidays, I felt waves of panic rise regularly and struggled to subdue them. For the first time in my life, I had insomnia and lived in a sleepless haze. Nicole worried about my health and got so frustrated with my lack of response to any of her questions that she gave up talking to me. With everyone on holiday, no one replied to my e-mails or calls and I felt powerless to move anything forwards.

In the first week back, I met Ralph Tabberer who was as worried about the situation as the rest of us, but luckily had been looking at options. Civil servants are often seen as inefficient or too wrapped up in bureaucracy, but at their best they are outstanding and make things happen. This was one of dozens of examples over the past decade when an official has helped ensure our success. He pointed me to a group of possible teaching colleges and universities, all of them high performers who would stand up well in any bidding process. He talked me through a list of key contacts in each institution, and one of them whom he thought might be interested – Professor Sonia Blandford.

Sonia was an educator with twenty years' experience as a teacher, school leader and educational reformer who had recently taken over as Dean of Education at what is now Canterbury Christ Church University. Ralph was convinced that the two of us would get along splendidly as we shared a great deal. He laughed about our similarities, describing Sonia as entrepreneurial, passionately focused on the issues of educational disadvantage, and completely bloody-minded.

We first met in mid-January, when Sonia and her colleagues came to London to bid for the training and size us up. We circled each other, trying to determine if we could work together. On the positive side, Ralph was right – she was a committed entrepreneur who made things happen – something often difficult to find in the education sector. Can you find accommodation for a 200-person residential course in six months' time? Yes. Can you design a teacher training programme from scratch? Yes. I asked if she could work according to the high standards that we were looking for and she gave me a withering look. It was clear that Sonia was not only skilled and experienced, but also got the plot. She shared our vision and values, which in retrospect was the most important thing we should have been looking for.

She made her bid subsequently and Canterbury won the contract on merit. With Sonia and her team on board, it felt like we finally had someone working with us to build the next stage of the programme. But, while it was great to have this support, part of me also worried about giving up ownership and control over such a large part of Teach First.

Sonia and her team busily got down to the work of designing a new, cutting-edge training programme with me and some of my team trying to influence it along the way. We quickly settled into a relationship of deep mutual respect, but also constant bickering. Sonia respected that these new teachers were expecting a different experience and that we understood them better than she did. She also respected our focus on the mission of addressing educational disadvantage and the need for leadership in schools where the majority of the pupils came from the lowest-income communities. Similarly, I respected her expertise and her can-do attitude. However, both of us were strong leaders who were not used to giving up control. In many ways, Ralph was correct. We were too alike – passionate, opinionated, and with strong self-belief. However, in other areas we were too different – by background, experience, knowledge and expertise. As a result, we struggled to come to agreement on how areas of the training would run, and who would be in charge of them.

Our first task was to recruit a team of tutors who could train and support our teachers. We agreed that we would only bring in people who both of us supported. This led to a number of vetoes on both sides (mostly on my side), but also to a mostly solid group of educators to joining us. We found an experienced London headteacher, Mary Wallis, who came on board to lead the team and won everyone's respect with her calm focus, maturity and warm smile. She brought an increased level of confidence to the entire programme. Then, Sonia attended a wedding one weekend and was so impressed with the best man's speech that, when she found out he was a teacher, asked him to help us out as a temporary employee that summer. He is still working with us ten years later as our head of training.

One of Sonia's colleagues proved particularly instrumental. A few weeks after Canterbury Christ Church came on board I was introduced to a grey-haired man in his sixties who had a youthful twinkle in his eye that belied his years. His name was James Learmonth and he had been a serious power broker in London education for decades as a school leader, inspector and judge for the national teaching awards. Having spent a large part of his career focused on the needs of inner-city children in London, he quickly became passionate about the impact that Teach First could make. He once told me of his hope that it could also prevent London schools from "poaching" teachers from less developed countries, which desperately needed them to solve their own educational disadvantage problems. He was adamant that the answer to solving London's difficulties lay in building good teaching and learning domestically, rather than endless tinkering with systems. I think he saw in us the possibility of building a base of professionals for deep change, rather than the quick fixes which were the staple of most politicians he had worked with.

Yet, with his strong reputation across the sector it was a brave decision of his to join this unproven scheme which most of the educational establishment was looking at with wary distrust. When he did come on board, he did not just dip his toe in the water, but dived into the deep end. He signed up as a consultant, but his role was much more than that – bringing us a great deal of credibility through a sort of quiet charisma that instilled confidence in people. It was inspirational to all of us that such a well-respected figure recognised and believed in the potential of Teach First even in the face of scepticism and some cynicism among many of his long-standing colleagues.

This encouraged others to suspend their judgement on Teach First and to begin to believe in our potential impact; and it brought on board new allies and collaborators, ensuring that, even with only a few months' lead time, our first summer institute and training year got our teachers ready for the rigours of their schools.

Within a few weeks of coming on board, James was diagnosed with cancer, something I, regrettably, barely acknowledged at the time as I focused single-mindedly on Teach First. Even with his illness, he continued to work passionately with us in between chemotherapy and surgery, making calls and sending e-mails from the hospital. At the time, I was so wrapped up in the day-to-day stresses that I probably did not appreciate his contribution, nor did I realise how ill he really was due to his boundless energy. Sometimes, I wonder if we would ever have been able to train and place that first group of teachers without his enormous commitment. It could have been just as likely for Teach First to have crashed and burned in its infancy as so many other start-ups do. In retrospect, we've been enormously lucky that throughout every part of the journey, the right sort of person seems to have come along to help us at the right time.

One of the most important leadership lessons I've learned is the need to be constantly on the lookout for this "step change" person to collaborate with to help us get to the next level – whether it be Jo, Rona, George, Ralph, Andrew, James Darley, Sonia or James Learmonth, or one of the others who have fulfilled that role.

Either way, it should have been clear to me by now that, with friends like this, we truly were no longer alone. This was a team effort. But just as I didn't fully appreciate James's contribution (or take notice of his rapidly declining health), I was still, all too often, only able to focus on the weight I felt on my own shoulders erroneously believing that everything was my personal responsibility.

As a result, I probably got involved in too much detail and often had vigorous disagreements with Sonia and others at the university where we would quickly ratchet up our differences into huffing and puffing and shouting. These ranged from the mundane (I wanted to make sure everyone ate together to build *esprit de corps*, while she felt it logistically impossible) to the developmental (I wanted more broad leadership training at the summer institute, while she pointed out that our teachers couldn't gain their qualification if they didn't have enough of a background in teaching pedagogy). Part of the problem was the cultural differences between the educators at the university and our management consultant mindset at Teach First. We both had a lot to learn from each other.

At one point, our disagreements reached a fevered pitch and we could not agree on how the summer institute days should be arranged or who should manage the tutors at different times. I was petrified that the institute would not push our "top graduates" enough or prepare them sufficiently for their work in the schools. It got to the point where we were perpetually angry at each other and weren't able to have civil conversations without them descending into tense arguments. At one point Sonia accused me of intentionally mispronouncing her name – calling her "Sooonya" as opposed to "Sonia". It really was just a result of my American accent, but I needed to sit down with Nicole for some "My Fair Lady"-style elocution lessons on how to pronounce this name with the proper British inflection.

We reached the stage where it was damaging the preparations for the summer and, in late-May, agreed on a summit meeting at Salomons in Tunbridge Wells, a large country estate mansion in Kent, where Sonia was attending a conference.

Sitting around a wooden table, surrounded by nineteenth-century oil portraits and overlooking beautifully landscaped gardens, it felt as far as possible from the schools and young people we were both so passionate

186

about supporting. Sonia and I, with some of our staff sitting next to us, worked through our disagreements with the tension of a nuclear treaty negotiation. Mary Wallis was in the middle taking notes and trying to bring us together. With a headteacher's precision and toughness, she reminded both of us of our focus on disadvantaged children and that if we couldn't figure out a way to collaborate successfully, they would be the ones to suffer. It was a useful conversation and helped us both back off from our confrontation.

This led to our real breakthrough, a pub dinner in Wapping the following week. After a few hours going through the curriculum for the summer institute, I suggested to Sonia that we have dinner at the Prospect of Whitby, the oldest river pub in London, just up the road from my flat. Over fish and chips and without anyone else around for whom we needed to keep up appearances, we bonded over our shared connection with the children we were hoping to help and some personal stories of our own childhoods. It was the first time we realised we could work together as individuals focused on a common vision, rather than enemies from "opposing" institutions. We managed to find a way to build our partnership, so much so that five years later, Sonia left her role at Canterbury to work as our Director of Leadership Development full time and is currently still a part-time adviser on our Senior Leadership Team. This has taught me the lesson that focusing on the end goal and a common mission is the best way to build successful partnerships and move beyond normal day-to-day bickering.

In addition to designing the training, the greatest hurdle

we had to overcome was actually convincing schools to hire these, as yet, unproven graduates. At the time, there was a teacher shortage in London, which was causing many schools to recruit from overseas, leading to high turnover. As one head told me "If all of these Australians went home, we'd have to shut down our school." Yet, even though there was a level of desperation about their recruitment problems, many of the headteachers were still difficult to convince. A number just could not get their heads around the idea that the teachers would start in the classroom after only six weeks' training, no matter how many times we explained the idea of the full two-year training and support they would receive. A few struggled with the whole concept, actually coming out and saying that they didn't think their pupils would respond well to top graduates (thankfully none of these people are still leading schools in London).

One technique we used at the meetings was to ensure that a Teach First employee was joined by one of our Canterbury allies who was respected by the school. James Learmonth was one such ally who was able to read a headteacher like a book and win him or her over based on his own substantial reputation.

At the same time, there were a number of forward-looking heads who positively leaped at the idea. One was Gill Bal, the newly appointed head of Wembley High Technology College, a low-performing school with a large proportion of pupils from low-income backgrounds with only 34% earning five good GCSEs and very few moving on to university. Gill had visionary ideas for where she wanted to take her school. She saw our teachers as the key to achieving it. When I visited her school, she had such a clear sense of where she wanted it to go and what was possible for her pupils that I was immediately impressed. She explained that there were sixty-eight languages spoken at Wembley "and that is wonderful, because it gives us something special to leverage." A few weeks earlier the school had gone through a period of serious behavioural issues, including the letting-off of fireworks in the building by a pupil (who, incidentially, was still at the school, because the school could not prove he done it). Even this she considered a potential blessing, as she saw it as an opportunity to set out a clear behaviour policy that could be consistently applied by all staff. She immediately asked me how many teachers she could take and we agreed to place eight in her school, a number that has continued for most of the past decade. In 2011, over 96% of her pupils gained at least five good GCSEs and almost all of her sixth-formers are now going to university, including places such as Oxford, Cambridge, UCL and Imperial College, a situation which would have been considered impossible when she took over the school.

Besides headteachers like Gill who positively embraced the programme, there were other heads who felt we were the least worse option, and others still who were talked into it by James or others at Canterbury; and little by little we managed to find teaching positions for all our new teachers that first year – another "impossible" task ticked off our "to do" list.

While all of these schools had a majority of their intake from low-income backgrounds, they had little else in common. Among the dozens of schools I visited that

189

first year, some operated in decaying urban centres, others in seemingly rural idylls right outside the M25. Some, like Wembley, were among the most multi-ethnic institutions outside of the United Nations, with ninety or more nationalities represented. Yet, others, only a few tube stations away, were based in some of the most monocultural places imaginable. There were centres of new immigrants and areas where third generation unemployment was the norm. I visited schools where the teachers worried about their children having enough to eat and I dined in others where the cafeteria served finer organic food than an expensive City restaurant. It has never ceased to amaze me just how difficult it is to stereotype what one of our schools looks like or what challenges the children within them face even within a single city such as London, much less throughout the whole of Britain.

By the end of June, though, it was time for our first summer institute and I boarded a train to Canterbury with a large suitcase to get me through the next six weeks. It was a great adrenaline rush to have 186 of the best graduates in the country joining together to be part of our team.

That night, the staff team and many of our new recruits went out for a drink at a pub on campus. Despite the vast challenges at the time, we all understood that we had pulled off a near miracle in bringing it together so quickly. As the soon-to-be-teachers milled around expectantly, flirting and sizing each other up, one of my team turned to me, "Brett, I think they're waiting for someone to say something. I think that's probably you." Unsure of what to do, and still nervous about public speaking, I stood up uncertainly. The room fell into an expectant silence, a really odd feeling as everyone turned from their conversations and pints to look at me. "Well, uh, hello!" I trembled with nervousness as I had never spoken to such a large group before. "Welcome everyone to Teach First. I think today is the start of something very special. You all are going to be building something that is going to change the face of education. Remember that. Let's all get a good night's sleep and the buses will take us to the morning meeting at 8am tomorrow! Congratulations to all of you on becoming the pioneers!" A cheer erupted, but my paternal advice was ignored. No one got a good night's sleep as the cohort closed the bar down that evening getting to know each other.

Years later, one of the graduates from that first intake admitted that much of their conversations there had centred on how old I was and where I was from. Everyone had assumed that, as leader of Teach First, I must be in my thirties or forties and thought I looked strangely youthful when they saw me at the bar. They also assumed I had to have been British, but when they heard me speak, the rumour was that I was Anglo-Canadian. Apparently there were bets going on all summer and by the end, a few worked up the nerve to ask me my age and find out who had won the competition by guessing I was a twenty-eight-year-old American. It was another reminder of my newly public stature that I was resolutely not used to.

The next afternoon, after registration, everyone gathered in the main lecture room at the university for the official opening ceremony. I think that more than any other day over the past ten years, this was the "oh my gosh" moment when all of us realised that we had created something very real that had great potential. As all of us on the staff team stood up front and watched the room fill up, buzzing with excitement, there was a collective realisation from that we had actually done what others said wasn't possible, and that this was only the start. There was no turning back. Within a few weeks these graduates had to be ready to teach in some of the most challenging classrooms of London. The bridge analogy popped back into my head. We had to get them to the other side of the ravine!

During the ceremony, we turned the lights down and played the throbbing beat from *The Matrix* as slides went up showing the scale of the problem and the impact we hoped they could make. It ended with a montage of their photos arranged to spell out the number 3,800,000. We had calculated that over the next two years, this group would have 3.8 million pupil interactions. Each one of these interactions was a leadership opportunity that they could take and it was up to them if it was going help address educational disadvantage or not. I read them a quote from the well-known American football coach Tom Landry that I thought summed up why we viewed great teachers as successful leaders, "Leadership is the ability to get a person to do what he doesn't want to do, or doesn't know he has to do, in order to achieve what he wants to achieve." I also introduced the cohort to the concept of "hills of happiness" and "valleys of death", by explaining the valleys we had been through to get to this stage and that it would be up to them to climb towards the hills of happiness past the valleys they would also no doubt experience. The analogy seemed to stick and it has continued to become a common feature in the language of Teach First over the past decade.

The next six weeks were a blur of long days, late nights, and constant fire-fighting. We had agreed that Canterbury would lead on the training from 9am to 5pm and that my team would lead the morning meetings from 8am to 9am and after 5pm. During the times we ran, we threw at the teachers all sorts of leadership memes, from Myers-Briggs testing, to army-led communications training, to more new age techniques, such as asking them to draw pictures of their own "territory" and leadership journey.

I would visit different classrooms during the day and what I saw ranged from shockingly bad (I heard one university tutor tell her charges: "Don't worry about doing too much your first year. Your school can't really expect that much of you and there's only so much you can do to help the pupils") to the truly brilliant and inspirational. At the time, there was a popular TV show called *Faking It* where people with no relevant experience would be chosen at random and trained for a week to do a high-profile job such as celebrity hairdresser, racing-car driver or interior decorator to the stars. They would only win if they could fool an expert on the last day of the week. Referencing this show became a theme of the cohort during the summer institute, with our soon-to-be teachers getting increasingly nervous about having to "fake it" in front of a real class in only a few weeks' time and jokingly looking for hidden cameras around Canterbury for the reality TV show stunt.

As Sonia and I tried to ensure that our teachers would be properly prepared and not have to fake it in the class-room, we tried to deal with the larger issue of defining what exactly our relationship was with them. On a small issue, I became incensed with the dress code. We were trying to create one of the most professional programmes in the country and I was dismayed to find not only our new teachers, but even our staff, wearing shorts and T-shirts at the institute. I cracked down on this and probably focused too much on the result rather than the underlying cause, which was that no one really knew what their role there actually was and how they should operate. There were just no norms. Were they students, professionals, colleagues or clients? The truth was that all of us often felt like we were faking it and weren't sure what persona we should be adopting. Were we leading them or were they leading us?

During the third week, the cohort moved to London to spend time in their placement schools.. Nerves abounded – this was the first time the heads would meet their new charges – but overall they did surprisingly well, taking charge of some classes during the final week of term and giving our partner schools a sense of security about what they would receive in the autumn. Our participants also felt slightly more secure after this week – now a known quantity, the pupils were slightly less scary. Yet, the scale of what they would have to face also became clearer. Everyone returned to Canterbury for the final three weeks with a renewed sense of purpose.

The night before our return, we were scheduled to have a celebratory event in London to mark the first anniversary of our launch. After weeks of lobbying the Prime Minister's Office and arranging for the event to be held at a venue and time amenable to his schedule, we achieved what at the time felt like another "impossible" triumph for a start-up charity – Tony Blair agreed to attend and address the guests. We had hundreds of our new teachers, business backers, employees and other supporters starting to arrive when I received a call from one of the Prime Minister's advisers with some bad news. Unfortunately, Tony Blair would not be able to attend our celebration. He had an important speech in Washington DC to prepare for instead. This turned out to be his famous speech to the joint houses of Congress later that week, where he accepted a Congressional Gold Medal and conveyed Britain's full and complete support to the United States in its upcoming military adventures in Iraq. I sometimes think, only somewhat facetiously, if future historians might consider this to be the moment when Tony Blair's premiership started to go down the wrong tracks – when the Prime Minister who campaigned on "education, education, education" started to focus too much of his energies on foreign entanglements instead.

We did get to meet Tony Blair a few months later when he opened the Business Academy in Bexley, tucked into the far southeast corner of London. The train ride to reach the school passed row upon row of Brutalist council estates that had been used to represent the dystopian future in *Clockwork Orange*. During his tour of the school, Blair made a visit to the classroom of one of our science teachers who had only been teaching for a few weeks. Our teacher was doing admirably as the scrum of officials and reporters entered his room. He calmly continued his lesson using an interactive white board, which was a new technology at the time, to show the effects of gravity on the orbit of planets and moons. To do this, he would flick his pointer on the board to control the speed of the spin of the planet. The animations on the board would then show the resulting effect on the orbit of the moons.

After explaining this to the class, he said he had a question for their distinguished guest and looked up at Tony Blair. Pointing to the planet on the white board, he asked, "Prime Minister, how much spin do you think we should put on this?" The reporters roared with laughter. After pausing a moment, Blair responded "Just a little spin, I think." The teacher promised me afterwards that he did not realise the double entendre of his question, but I still don't believe him.

While we never did get Blair to meet all of our teachers, we were fortunate to have a young Shadow Secretary of Education, David Cameron, visit a subsequent summer institute.

During a morning assembly, I mentioned to our teachers that a member of the Conservative front bench was visiting us for the day. The room erupted in boos. However, after a half-day visit, during which Cameron had "listening meetings" with our teachers, staff and university tutors in small groups and then gave a speech followed by a long Q&A, he received an ovation from our cohort. He had successfully "detoxified" his party for our young graduates in only a few hours.

Impressed with his communication skills, I placed a £20 bet at Ladbrokes later that day that he would become the next party leader at 5 to 1 odds – the first and only time I've placed a political bet in my life.

HOW TO SUCCEED AGAINST THE ODDS
The Bethnal Green Academy story

Bethnal Green Academy educates pupils from one of the most deprived boroughs in the country but in 2011, 80% of the pupils there achieved five A*– C grades (including English and Maths) with 98% of pupils getting five A*– G grades.

The figures seem even more incredible when you realise that only four years ago just 34% of pupils achieved this, the school was in special measures and months away from being closed down; and 75% of pupils have English as an additional language with over thirty principal languages spoken.

The school, which until recently was known as Bethnal Green Technology College, has been home to Teach First participants since 2004, with between four to five new participants coming through the gates every year since. Our teachers have tended to stay on after their second year with current ambassadors in their third, fourth and fifth year of teaching, some of whom are members of the senior leadership team.

Headteacher Mark Keary arrived in 2006 when the third cohort was beginning and was immediately impressed by what he saw.

Mark says: "When they finish their first year and become Newly Qualified Teachers we give them a role that is based on a whole school experience rather than just the classroom so we are pushing them hard to expand their experience."

Back in 2006 Teach Firster Kate Jarman came to Mark with a plan to do something about the school's lack of community cohesion and prevalent gang culture, which included a lot of racially motivated violence. Kate was just starting her second year on Teach First and felt very passionately about the importance of citizenship as a course on the curriculum. Having voiced her feelings to Mark, he gave her the challenge of coming up with a course in only four weeks which would be rolled out to the whole school the following term.

Mark says: "It was a ridiculous challenge but Kate rose to it and pulled a fantastic course together. It has been one of the things that has improved the way the pupils interact with each other and their community." Kate now works at the Department for Education as an adviser where she has been for three years.

Mark also cites Tessa Blair as another inspirational Teach First recruit. Currently the assistant headteacher and head of professional learning for new trainee teachers, Tessa has developed a programme which is based on class practice rather than theory with continual evaluation and coaching.

"It is far more authentic as you need to be practical in teaching and the impact is seen straight away in the classroom," Mark says. "The learning is outcome based and has been a huge success with people making unbelievable progress and being promoted to heads of faculty."

Almost the entire humanities department is Teach First and has been yielding phenomenal results. Recently, English teacher Kiran Gill organised a performance of *Romeo and Juliet* for her pupils, which was performed at a West End theatre. Mark says: "The children learnt so much from her, their self-confidence rocketed which has had a ripple effect on others.

"The school recently won an Education and Business award for Outstanding Progress and I was amazed when the pupils who attended with me started discussing their favourite Shakespearian speeches during the quieter periods of the event."

Mark wants to offer more arts and music in the school as well as improving on the academic results and sees Teach First as being an essential part of this.

"We are still the only developed country in the world where educational achievement is defined by the postcode of origin and that needs to change as it's not right," he says. "If it hadn't been for the first cohort of Teach First participants and the regular influx of enthusiasm that comes with them every year, along with their madcap ideas which often change the way we do things, we wouldn't be where we are now. I hope that Teach First is around for many years to come."

The final weeks of the summer institute continued to speed by with full intensity until the final afternoon in mid-August when Sonia and I presented completion certificates to the cohort. Later that evening, at an all-night costume party organised by our teachers. I danced in a Che Guevara costume, cigar firmly clenched in my mouth, thinking of how very wrong my colleague had been those many months earlier when he had said revolutions didn't happen in Britain. *Viva la revolución*!

All of us went to bed deliriously happy that night, satisfied that another milestone was behind us. However, when I woke up the next morning, I discovered once again how quickly valleys and hills can follow each other. Sonia called with an uncharacteristically panicked voice. James Learmonth had passed away from his cancer overnight. After providing near constant support throughout the previous months, one of his last acts had been to send a supportive e-mail to a sceptical headteacher the evening before.

There is a Talmudic belief that even a single blade of

grass needs to have its own angel that bends over it and whispers, "grow, grow" in order for it to reach its potential. Over the years, Teach First has had many such angels. One of my regrets is that I haven't always appreciated what sacrifices they've made to nurture our green shoots, particularly during our early years. It is an important lesson for all growing organisations to remember.

Once our teachers started in September, we continued to develop our support structure, while trying to calibrate our expectations of them and those that they should have of their students. It's a struggle we've continued to have every year since – how to balance humility with high expectations.

HOW TO LEAD

Teach First believes the qualities underpinning excellent teaching are the same as those underpinning excellent leadership. If you don't understand teaching as a leadership role, it is easy to limit it. We are looking for classroom leaders with an entrepreneurial spirit, who are highly flexible and adaptive and able to find a way through for each pupil regardless of the challenges they are facing.

They should be entering each class asking the questions "where do we need to go and how will we get there?" before diving into things. While subject knowledge is extremely important, equally crucial for many of the young people in Teach First schools is for their teachers to help them, in Antoine de Saint-Exupéry's sublime phrase, to "yearn for the vast and endless sea" and give them the academic tools to build the ship themselves.

Great leaders can be catalysts for positive change and their results are clearly demonstrable. To be successful, like any good leader, our teachers have to become credible very quickly. To help facilitate this, Teach First's leadership focus has constantly been evolving, based on evidence, so that we can increase our impact on young people each year. Perhaps this is one of the most important principles of leadership – having the integrity to evaluate what works and to be on the look-out constantly to ratchet up your effectiveness.

As of 2012, our leadership focus comprises three strands – Leading Learning, Leading People and Leading Self. Each strand is designed to develop leadership knowledge, skills and mindsets which will enable our teachers to lead change in addressing educational disadvantage, both during their initial two years and long-term, no matter where their career takes them. During their initial two years in the classroom, Leading Learning is the core strand of the programme, with the other two as supporting strands. This strand has five main principles, which we believe are relevant for all leaders:

1. Having a strong vision

Effective leaders have high expectations of those who follow them and effective teachers have high expectations of their students, with a clear vision about how each of them is going to develop over the course of a year. The greatness of the teaching must be relative to the vision for that classroom and the needs of those students. Visions exist to hold teachers and students to account, to inform the way lessons are taught each day, and the work students complete. We ask our teachers to be prepared to have a vision that is related to student need based on raising their levels of Achievement, Access and Aspirations.

2. Sharing the vision and collaborating with others

Collaboration is key to the realisation of any leadership vision. Collaboration with parents, carers and colleagues who all play crucial roles in the student's education. Sharing the vision and finding ways to build on the leadership that others are providing in the child's life will motivate everyone to help make it happen.

3. Creating a great environment

In order for leaders to maximise their ability to achieve a vision, it is essential that they build an environment conducive to supporting this. In schools, students need to be provided with an environment which enables learning. Effective teachers give their students the opportunity to share their views, share in each other's successes and demonstrate that they also believe all children can achieve – creating a sense of joyful love of learning. Establishing an efficient, well-behaved classroom sets the tone that students are there to learn and that the teacher's expectations must be met. This then enables better attainment results for the young people.

4. Planning strategically and delivering effectively

For a leader to reach their ambitious goals, it is crucial to plan strategically and deliver effectively. In the classroom, this means using a deep understanding of students' strengths and needs to feed into planning and to determine what will be taught, when it will be taught, and how it will be delivered to achieve the best results for the pupils. Great leaders constantly look for innovative ways to engage students in their learning and help them leave the class with an enduring understanding of the subject. Teachers need to see themselves as leaders whose actions have a direct impact on their students' attainment.

5. Being reflective and solutions-focused

The practice of reflection is crucial to the development of all effective leaders, but especially in a classroom environment where the learning curve is so steep for new teachers. Great teachers need to adapt and adjust their approach all the time to ensure that the pupils are learning and successfully working towards a shared vision. Constant reflection enables great leaders to identify both their successes and areas of improvement so that they can continue to improve.

Overall, our trainee teachers did well during that first year. They all faced different challenges in convincing their colleagues, and their pupils, of their fitness for their role. Often, they over-exaggerated their age to their pupils so that they wouldn't be thought of as inexperienced. Very few actually identified themselves as Teach First teachers to their classes. This posed a potential problem for two of them whom we picked to feature on a BBC news segment during their first week in school. The piece showed them preparing their lesson plans while a narrator relayed in a concerned voice, "these two women are unqualified teachers who have only had six weeks' training. Many in the teaching profession think they shouldn't be allowed to teach. Yet, they feel ready." To their horror, some of their students saw the segment and reminded them of their lack of experience frequently. We learned a valuable PR lesson.

During that first year, we worked with our inaugural cohort to determine what they could achieve in the classroom and how we could best support them to achieve it. But unsure what we were looking for, it was difficult for us to know how best to support them. We threw a number of different ideas together, which included coaches from the private sector, school mentors, school project competitions and summer internships.

One idea, that Jo Owen came up with, was the holding of periodic "Cock-Up Clubs". We believed that one of the core competencies of leadership was the ability to climb out of the valleys of death that our teachers were experiencing during some difficult lessons. As a result, we had the idea of introducing them to great leaders in business, policy, charity and education who would talk about their biggest valleys of death, or "cock-ups", and how they got through them. These have proven to be inspiring learning experiences for our teachers. Some of the cock-ups shared by FTSE 100 CEOs and well-known policy leaders – including stories of losing £100 million due to an inputting mistake, designing a marketing strategy that failed miserably and even dating a boss as an office junior – have helped put our teachers' day-to-day difficulties in perspective. It's an important lesson that "this too shall pass" and that great leaders find a way to overcome even the greatest mistakes and difficulties and constantly improve. It has proven crucial for our teachers, who have to learn both how to recover from less successful lessons themselves and how to pass this example of resilience onto their pupils.

In the meantime, the university tutors were working with our teachers through fortnightly visits and twice-termly subject training days. Their job was to ensure that our teachers had the necessary skills to be successful in the classroom and gain Qualified Teacher Status, through observations and written evidence that they met all of the standards necessary for qualification.

It was a challenge to ensure everyone was completely aligned – particularly on the issue of the importance of instilling a sense of urgency among our teachers and ensuring they had high expectations of their students. We heard examples of one tutor telling our teachers "well, you can't expect too much from such a difficult class" or that some thought it was impossible to expect a teacher to be successful in such a tough school. At the same time, other tutors were inspirational, supporting our teachers to constantly grow in their expectations of their students and themselves. This difference in messaging and beliefs caused a great deal of tension for all of us and a great deal of confusion among our teachers.

One problem we faced was that the university and Teach First cultures were so different. All of the Teach First employees were in their twenties, while the average university tutor's age was closer to fifty. We were a radical, impatient lot, while they had seen lots of young people and trainee teachers in their years and felt they understood schools much better than us. Sonia and I struggled to figure out how the two teams, coming from such different cultures, could work effectively together.

We solved this problem in a number of ways – through lots of conversations and joint tutor-assessment that Sonia and I led, as well as more clearly defining our expectations of our teachers and all of their support structures. However, there were still problems. There were instances of Teach First and university employees talking negatively about each other, with our teachers caught in the middle.

We knew we needed to do something radical to bring everyone together. As I started to plan our second annual three-day employee offsite, I suggested a radical concept – how about if we invited all of the Canterbury tutors to join us so that we could surface and work through these differences? Sonia quickly agreed.

We held the offsite at Keble College in Oxford. Amid the beautifully landscaped quadrangles and gorgeous Victorian Gothic chapel and library that oozed a feeling of "relaxed academic excellence", it was difficult to imagine that there could be any problems. Yet, the first two days were extraordinarily tense and angry. Many of the university tutors wanted to spend their time alone, focused on "real" training to prepare for their school visits, rather than talking about namby-pamby ideas like vision and values. As I talked about our mission, what we were trying to achieve, and the importance of high expectations, one tutor pointedly asked me in front of everyone, "And what do you think we're trying to achieve? I've spent forty years working with young people, helping them to be successful. What do you and your business friends know about what happens in a classroom!" I stood there through the assault, feeling personally attacked, and wishing for the ground to swallow me up, but also, deep in my consciousness, realising she had a point. She was exactly the sort of person we needed to collaborate with and win over in order to make real system change possible.

After two exhausting days of what felt to me like constant personal abuse, all I wanted to do was crawl home, and into Nicole's arms, but that evening we had planned a social event – a black-tie dinner in the college's hall, followed by a dance. I had enthusiastically pushed this idea, convinced that it could help us break down barriers and get to know each other better – with the formal dress forcing us onto our best behaviour. However, as we sat down, I worried that this would be one of my all-time worst ideas, down there with agreeing to attend a paint ball competition with the staff a few months earlier, which had degenerated into welts all over my body as everyone trained their guns on me. I thought about feigning illness to avoid having to attend.

It started as a miserable evening. Throughout the dinner, everyone was grumpy with each other, and especially with me for putting them through this awkward encounter. The two groups sat as far apart as possible, just hoping for the night to quickly go by so that they could get to bed. The beginning of the dance reminded me of a group of twelve-year-olds at their first co-ed social, with the two very different cliques barely daring to look at each other and wondering when it would be polite to leave.

Finally, one of the tutors, David Wasp, a former London headteacher and schools inspector in his sixties with a warm smile and a hugely positive manner came forwards. He normally walked with a cane, but this time he put it down and started – very slowly, but also very deliberately – to boogie with two of the Teach First team who were on the dance floor. Soon, some of the women on our team started dancing with him and a number of his colleagues also joined. Within a little while, everyone was dancing and chatting and treating each other more like colleagues and less like adversaries. Perhaps the open bar also helped.

While bringing together such disparate cultures

continues to be a long-term project, it felt like real progress had been made by the time we left on day three. There was better communication from that point forwards and somehow, perhaps because in reality almost all of us were working towards the same goal, we began to feel a little bit more like a team. We needed each other and couldn't do it alone. In the end, it wasn't really the dancing or the alcohol, or the offsite that brought us together. It was the children and young people we were all trying to help.

Over the next nine years, we continued to develop this training partnership and, as we grew, brought in more partners. Soon, we were working with fourteen universities on our teacher training, as well as over forty businesses, dozens of charities, three business schools, and over 500 schools. This level of collaboration has often been difficult. Building a common culture with such a disparate group and ensuring we are working towards a common vision is a continuous work-in-progress.

In the summer of 2011, the national Office of Standards in Education, or Ofsted, sent inspectors across the country to hold a full independent evaluation of Teach First's training with our university partners, randomly picking on Teach First classrooms and participants to examine. On the Friday afternoon of the final day of the inspection, my senior team and I waited expectantly in our offices to meet with the lead inspector and discover the team's findings.

He started the meeting by noting that he usually made sure to sit nearest the exit when delivering final inspection reports in case he needed to make a quick getaway. With a smile, he assured us that he didn't expect that would be necessary in this instance.

Our focus on continual improvement had paid off. The inspectors gave the training its highest possible grade of "Outstanding" in all forty-four areas evaluated across all the regions that Teach First was operating in. Crucially, the final report stated that "Teach First is very successful in meeting its commitment to address educational disadvantage." It noted that our retention of teachers "is exceptionally high" and "significantly above the national average", while confirming that we recruit a "diverse cohort with a high proportion nationally of participants from a wide range of minority ethnic backgrounds".

It closed with the finding that pleased me most of all. "The attainment of participants is outstanding and has improved each year for the last three years... As a result of the quality of the training they receive and their own ability to critically reflect, the overwhelming majority of participants make outstanding progress against highly challenging expectations, meeting or exceeding these expectations."

We know that this still isn't good enough. The challenges many of our young people face are so great that they are not yet attaining the levels they are capable of.

However, there can be no doubting the power of a great classroom leader who, within a wider system of collaborative support, can lead young people towards ever higher levels of achievement, aspiration and access to opportunity.

Working together has paid great dividends. What we've seen over the past decade is that these graduates can be trained and supported to successfully teach those children – they just can't do it alone.

Abdullah

Abdullah is a clever thirteen-year-old who shows enormous academic potential, during the few times that he actually shows up in class. Most of the time, he is a truant, often working as a "Younga" (a junior lookout for a gang based in his council estate), who has to do whatever is necessary to ensure that drug deals are not disrupted. His parents, recent immigrants from Somalia, don't know what to do. They left civil war and risked everything to give him more opportunities, but aren't sure how to change his behaviour. His mother has to take care of his five younger siblings. His father works fourteen hours a day. They come to our teacher begging for help. What can they do to help him understand the importance of education when so many other social factors are pulling him in an opposite direction? Should they beat him? Throw away his trainers and Playstation? Lock him in his room? Our teacher, who is only half their age, works through an alternative solution with them. Abdullah's father will walk him to school on his way to work each morning. Our teacher will arrive at 7am (school starts at 8.30) to meet him at the gate and they will eat breakfast together. After school, Abdullah will stay and do his homework, observed by our teacher who will then walk him home at 5pm. Within a few weeks of this routine, Abdullah is flourishing and achieving at the top of his class. Yet, the gangs are pursuing him relentlessly and our teacher worries – what will happen during summer break when no one is around to protect him from them?

5

"*Britain doesn't 'do' movements*"
The Value of Leadership

I was standing on the twenty-third floor of the Shell Centre near Waterloo Station overlooking the Thames dressed in an airline captain's outfit with "flight attendants" directing traffic and checking passports on either side of me. "Praise You" by Fat Boy Slim was blaring over the speakers and I started feeling uncomfortably like an extra in a Cher video.

It was July 2005 and Teach First's inaugural cohort had just finished their two-year commitment to their schools. All of them had come together for their graduation, but we had a little surprise for them. It wasn't actually going to be a graduation at all – that would imply that they had completed their obligations and, in reality, they hadn't even come close. Educational disadvantage still existed. Our job had not been done. Yet, they deserved a celebration and a way to mark the next stage of their journey. As a result,

211

they were getting on a "flight" to take them on a voyage of discovery. When they landed, they would have arrived at the next stage of their role as officially appointed Teach First ambassadors – a new term we had invented to signify their role in continuing to champion the vision that they had been working towards.

When I was developing the original business plan for Teach First, which included the importance of long-term leadership to solve this problem, some people said to me that Britain doesn't "do" movements – defined as a mass group from all levels of society engaged in a series of actions or activities intended towards a particular end. I was told authoritatively that the idea seemed much more French or American at a pinch, in tune with their more revolutionary cultures, with the US civil rights movement as an often-cited example. While the United States, as de Tocqueville first observed in 1835, is a nation of community organisers, in Britain, I was told, things evolve naturally and slowly. Even in modern times, Britain has little history of large-scale active alumni movements, in contrast to the United States where university affiliation has historically fostered a deep and life-long sense of connection.

In reality, though, this is a misreading of British history, as some of the greatest injustices in the country's past have been overturned through the bravery of movements of ordinary citizens at all levels of society putting themselves on the line, rather than as a result of top-down decisions by elites – for instance, the mass of petitioners in the early nineteenth century who helped end the slave trade and the individuals at all levels of society who led the women's suffragette movement early in the twentieth.

I believed that there was a similar courageousness among forward-looking individuals in the early twenty-first century who would dedicate themselves to ending the plague of educational disadvantage – a situation that seems as impossible to end today as the disadvantages of earlier eras seemed to those societies.

Creating a movement of individuals working together to lead change in education was always a core part of the plan behind Teach First. The scale of the injustice in schools serving low-income communities was so great that a small number of new teachers would never be able to make a dent in the situation. Instead, we needed our participants to join the ground swell of people working to address the problem and for all of them to continue to effect change in their classrooms, schools and throughout the system. The idea was that after spending two years focused on raising the achievement, aspirations and access of their children in their classrooms, our participants would never be able to let go of the need to solve this problem.

In many ways, we were uniquely placed to build this sort of movement. According to academic literature of what affects alumni engagement, there are six elements that a programme needs to have to strengthen long-term commitment from their alumni.[5] We had all of them: the core programme is more than a year long (check); the experience is highly intense (definitely check); the programme accepts less than 50% of applicants (18% for Teach First, check); the participants are more than eighteen years old in their initial placement (check); the participants have had similar previous life experiences (check for us, if you

5. "Non Profits' Untapped Resources", McKinsey Quarterly, February 2004.

include the competencies and values we select for); and the programme hosts the participants for at least part of the time (check, if you include the residential summer institute). As a result, Teach First should be able to develop a long-term connection with its alumni. Underlying all of this has been the common mission of "addressing educational disadvantage" that we select for and the common values of Commitment, Collaboration, Excellence, Integrity and Leadership that we model, which provide the shared language for everyone involved – and a strong platform to build a movement for change.

We quickly realised that the core of building a movement for change was for our cohorts of teachers and their colleagues to take to heart the value of leadership. Only if they had a personal sense of possibility for what children from low-income communities were capable of and a personal sense of responsibility for ensuring these young people's success, would true change be able to occur. It was about moving people from believing that solving this issue was outside of their locus of control to helping them understand that they were critical to the solution. It was about empowering them to create a movement that would *lead* the necessary change. As American anthropologist Margaret Mead once said, "Never doubt that a small group of thoughtful, committed citizens can change the world; indeed, it's the only thing that ever has". If they could be strong enough leaders, working collaboratively with others focused on the same vision, then anything would be possible.

We tried to set this vision up among our first cohort from the start, but probably focused too much on the first two years of teaching – no doubt because our organisational constraints didn't allow us to plan more than one step ahead. As a result, we didn't sufficiently help them prepare to stay engaged with the mission for the rest of their careers, whether or not they continued to teach in the classroom. This "non-graduation" graduation event at the Shell Centre in 2005 with its focus on a flight from one destination to another was our way to sharpen this focus.

The room was set up like a runway, with all the employees dressed in flight attendant outfits. Each teacher was given a passport when they arrived, which they then had to fill out on where they would go next on their journey. They each wrote down how they believed they would continue to work on helping the education of children in challenging circumstances. We then spent some time talking about the take-off (the past two years); the flight turbulence (some of their valleys of death) and their biggest successes (hills of happiness). We then landed. As they left, they had their passports stamped to become an ambassador for the next stage of the journey. The analogy got a bit forced at times, but it was a really powerful event that achieved just the right balance of celebration and sense of purpose.

A few months earlier, I had been worried that too many people (including some of our employees and first cohort) still saw Teach First as a two-year programme focused on filling teacher vacancies – a deficit model approach that fits into an easy narrative, but one I had always tried hard to dispel. It was clear that, in my nightmare analogy, I hadn't yet built the bridge strong enough to get all of our first cohort completely over the ravine to where they were equipped, inspired, and connected to lead long-term change.

As a result, I took the risky decision at that point of using the funding I had earmarked for hiring a finance director to hire a director of alumni instead. The result was that, though we had a programme of support all ready for the first cohort when they finished their two years, we also had a few years of nail-biting audits and poor financial reporting. In retrospect, the right decision would have been to have fundraised twice as much and hired both crucial positions. While I correctly prioritised our programmatic strength, I made the common entrepreneurial mistake of under-prioritising our operational strength. These are important lessons that I've promised to remember if I ever create another new enterprise.

The person who we brought on board to lead our alumni work, Sarah Higgs (now Sarah Connor), was an experienced teacher who had also worked for the BBC and as the managing partner of a communications agency focusing on brand and strategy development for the not-for-profit sector. One of her first acts in post was to change her title to Director of Ambassadors and to think through how we could signify this change as part of the "non-graduation" event. It was all part of a wider piece of work on how we could instil more of a feeling of leadership among the cohort.

During our first few years, I saw an uncomfortable "parent/child" relationship that seemed to develop between central Teach First staff and our teachers, which undermined the central leadership goal of the programme. This probably started during our first summer institute when the new participants came in not knowing what to expect and our employees led the sessions. I worried that each side sometimes did not show enough respect for the work that the other was doing. This could become apparent when employees sent e-mails or texts "telling off" the participants who were not attending Teach First events they were supposed to, or when some of our teachers acted like children at the events – showing up late or chatting among themselves while Teach First partners were leading sessions.

I tried to think of ways to change this dynamic. One idea was to hire in a new ambassador from among our teachers in a short-term role to help break down barriers and ensure we were all working together towards a common vision.

There was no funding for yet another position, but I was convinced that we needed to create a continuous improvement culture that constantly modelled self-evaluation and humility. I believed that the best way for us to show this was to ensure that there was someone constantly holding us to account for internal improvements and bringing in fresh thinking. As a result, I wrote a job description for a new one-year position, which I at first tentatively called "Manager of Programme Improvement". Then, thinking that this didn't sound like the exciting and powerful leadership role I envisioned, boldly changed the name to "Participant President" and rashly decided to make our twentieth full-time, paid, staff position one that was elected by our teachers rather than appointed by me or another member of my team.

This faced opposition internally, with many of our

employees rightly making the point that there were no assurances that our teachers would elect someone suitable for the role.

We were giving up control over the appointment and, with our meagre resources so precious, the role might not pay off. I wanted to make the Participant President accountable to their fellow teachers and not the "corporate" organisation, so there was the risk that their priority could become making a list of demands on how Teach First participants should be treated, rather than being focused on our ultimate vision. Yet, I stood firm. Only if this person had some sort of personal mandate would they feel empowered to serve as a conduit for our community. Also, I felt it sent a powerful signal – we trusted them and in exchange expected them to lead. Our teachers needed to be given some authority if we were expecting such great responsibility from them.

In January 2005, I sent a note out to all of our teachers, explaining that "I strongly believe that you are the leaders of Teach First. You will decide whether Teach First is an interesting experiment about filling vacancies for two years in some London schools, or is a long-term movement that radically reduces educational disadvantage nationwide and continues to attract the country's future leaders. The Teach First Participant President position is an opportunity for you to impact directly on the strategic direction of the organisation. By nominating, electing and/or standing for this position you will decide how Teach First should improve in the coming year to meet our goals, which many would say are impossible."

We had three strong candidates who received enough

nominations to get on the ballot and answered the detailed questions in the manifesto form that we asked them to fill out. We then held a hustings event where our teachers quizzed the three of them on what improvements they would like to see in the programme (most popular responses included tighter communications guidelines and better sharing of best teaching practices among the cohort). It was a tough, hard-fought election, but the winner – James Townsend – started on staff that August after he finished his second year teaching.

In many ways, it changed the mood of the team. With a few other early participants who joined our staff, some important classroom experience was brought on board and ensured that everything we were doing was grounded in the day-to-day reality of our teachers. We have kept the job going in the years since and it has proven an important leadership role that has received a great deal of interest from our cohorts.

FROM THE PRESIDENCY TO THE PIGSTY
Ruth's story

All the Participant Presidents have fulfilled their leadership roles in different ways – including representing their peers in meetings with royalty, prime ministers, CEOs and overseas visitors. They have helped implement new ideas, gauge the mood music on the ground, and sometimes give difficult feedback to everyone involved at Teach First – including myself.

After their year in the role, they have gone on to do an

assortment of things, including staying on Teach First staff, returning to teaching, or moving to other charitable organisations.

One of the most interesting next steps was taken by our 2007/8 Participant President, Ruth Carney, who decided to continue her role in the movement as one of a growing number of social entrepreneurs focused on creating new ways to work towards our vision that no child's educational success is limited by their socio-economic background.

A religious education teacher in a large, multi-cultural school close to Heathrow Airport, Ruth found her first year in teaching incredibly hard and began to understand that 'challenge' was specific to each school context. For Ruth, teaching RE in an urban school presented frustrations and joys in almost equal measure.

Ruth would have stayed on as a teacher in her school if she hadn't been elected by her peers to be the third Participant President, and the first woman to hold the position. She joined us in 2007 at a time of rapid expansion. We'd recently moved to Manchester and were expanding the northwest region while also launching in the West Midlands. There were those among the participant population who felt that we were expanding too quickly and that we should slow down and consolidate our activity. Ruth played a key role in helping communicate to participants the case for expansion: the problem was too urgent for us to stop now. At the same time, she continued to stress to all of us the importance of ensuring a quality intake to meet the huge challenges that go with working in a Teach First school, and in improving the support we gave our new teachers.

During her year as president of a now national programme, Ruth got a real sense of what disadvantage looked like throughout England, which further fuelled her commitment to tackling this issue in the long-term. She also met Jamie Feilden, a member of our inaugural 2003 cohort who was working in our graduate recruitment team, having taught history in Croydon.

While teaching, Jamie had noticed his children had little understanding of life outside of their neighbourhoods. As an experiment, he brought two sheep from his family's farm in Bath to graze next to the school's playground – and noted how some of the most disengaged children in his class thrived from the responsibility of feeding and caring for the animals. While working for us, he then joined up with Teach First partner schools and other Teach First participants to pilot a scheme for bringing groups of school pupils to the farm where, he says, the experience of living and working in the countryside gave the most vulnerable students a new purpose and direction in their lives.

Ruth also got excited about this concept and worked with Jamie to start the Jamie's Farm project, taking children at risk of exclusion from Teach First schools on regular trips to Jamie's family farm. Here they worked with Tish Feilden, Jamie's mother, a psychotherapist who had over thirty years experience of working with children in schools, and together developed a distinct educational and therapeutic methodology aimed at preventing vulnerable children from being excluded from school.

At the Teach First Conference in October 2007, Jamie first pitched the project to of Teach First ambassadors to drum up interest and feedback. This was followed by features about Jamie's Farm on the ambassadors' website, and e-newsletters asking ambassadors to volunteer to support visits. Inspired by support from Teach First colleagues, in 2008, Jamie and Ruth left Teach First to establish Jamie's Farm as a charity – Jamie as CEO and Ruth as COO.

> Now, Jamie's Farm works with a growing network of Teach First teachers from over forty schools, while a large number of ambassadors volunteer to fundraise and support visits.
>
> By 2012, they had expanded to a permanent site to work with nearly 500 children a year, providing a unique combination of 'farming, family and therapy' through a short stay residential and follow-up programme.
>
> Their results are excellent. One year later, over two-thirds of the children on the programme are no longer at risk of exclusion. Ruth, meanwhile, continues to believe that national change is possible. Even with all of her good work at Jamie's Farm, her proudest moment was recently seeing two of her former students join the Teach First programme – a great 'virtuous circle' that she hopes will continue, enabling the movement to grow and flourish and affect ever more young people.

The second idea to strengthen their ownership of Teach First among our teachers was one that I developed with our new chair, Dame Julia Cleverdon, the following year. Dame Julia was appointed to the role in June 2006 as part of our work to develop a stronger governance model that would enable us to grow beyond our start-up phase. She had been involved with Teach First since before the beginning, having helped organise the original Highgrove event which led to the McKinsey work and then serving as one of the co-clients for the team. Listed in *The Times* as one of the fifty most influential women in the UK, she had been CEO of Business in the Community since 1992 and was uniquely placed to have the ear of business leaders, charity heads and politicians of all stripes – as well as serving as one of HRH Prince Charles's most trusted advisers on charitable work.

She combined all of this with a warm, informal, irreverent style and an entrepreneur's focus on madly ambitious goals, even if achieving them sometimes required cutting corners around well-established norms – two personality traits that quickly endeared her to me. She also taught me a great deal about the collaborative effort needed to build a movement. As she posited when she was appointed, "Brett, for Teach First to really succeed, you and I need to become like Torville and Dean [the 1984 Olympic ice dancing gold medallists]. One of us lifts, while the other twirls, but if we can do it in unison, we'll get world class results." The analogy was apt. I've learned over the years what a valuable role a strong relationship between chair and CEO can play in building a successful organisation and ensuring coordinated external messages and strategy.

Dame Julia and I soon developed this relationship based on a common vision for Teach First and the movement of leaders we wanted to empower, as well as frequent dinners and chats. As we set about building a strong board, one of the innovations we agreed on was to appoint two ambassadors as trustees. Although they were less than half of the age of most of the other members, who had had decades of distinguished service in business, education and policy, they would help to keep the conversations "real" and also serve as a powerful link with the rest of the ambassadors. It would also send a significant message of empowerment to our teachers – this is your movement to lead, so much so that some of you are legal owners of this charity and are therefore effectively the executive's boss.

I also worked to build this sense of a movement at the summer institutes. On these six-week residential courses we worked with the participants 24/7, encouraging them – as part of their training – to feel like leaders and to work towards achieving the vision.

As their first year came to a close, one of the ways we decided to ingrain this idea was to have the participants return to the summer institute, but this time in the role of "teacher" rather than "trainee". They would spend a few days working with the new recruits – explaining how they had raised attainment in their classes. This has become their final task in order to gain Qualified Teacher Status. It has proven to be one of the most powerful ways to strengthen the idea of "teaching as learning" and an *esprit de corps* among all our participants.

I've always found these days and the "inter-cohort" training among the most inspiring events at Teach First. There is something wonderful about seeing the personal growth in the second-year teachers – watching them having developed from nervous new graduates into established professionals after only eleven months in the classroom. It's also an excellent growth experience for our new trainee teachers to understand the difficulties ahead of them and to see what great leadership goals they can aim for in even their first year. I get enormously excited about seeing hundreds (and now close to 2000) of the Teach First participants all together in one room, buzzing with energy and the belief that they can change the world.

Addressing this group is one of my favourite tasks. However, sometimes I do go a bit overboard, and did so spectacularly during our third summer institute in 2005.

I had married Nicole a few months earlier, in April, after three years of her providing the emotional partnership necessary for me to carry on through the difficult early days of Teach First. That July, I proudly invited Nicole and my new in-laws down to Canterbury to visit the big event where we had all of our Teach Firsters working together. They sat at the back as I got on stage and prepared to address the more than 400 new and experienced teachers there who had already spent a few hours working together. Barely able to contain my excitement, I started my speech: "I am so excited to be here. This is always my favourite day of the year, and this year is no exception. I can't tell you how great it is to see all of you working together and building this great movement for change. It really is the highlight of my entire year. I can't think of anything better than this!" I don't think Nicole (or her parents, who paid for most of our wedding) have yet forgiven me.

This has taught me the importance of keeping a wider perspective on, for the lack of a better term, "work/life balance". Leading Teach First has been an intense activity over the years, but I have found that setting boundaries has also been important. Although I am often travelling during the week, I always make sure to get home early on Fridays and spend Saturdays completely off e-mails and the internet to focus on my family. I have taken my full holiday allowance each year and recommend others on my team do the same. I would tell all of our teachers that it is important periodically to take a step back in order to have the energy to continue to focus on our work. Finally,

Sunday night has been enshrined as "Date Night" for Nicole and myself.

My focus on the summer institutes has continued, though. I have moved each summer to live at the institute, with Nicole (and now our children) often joining me there. Partly this is a selfish decision – I absolutely love being in the thick of things and reconnecting with our teams and our teachers. The manic residential aspects also bring back some of my favourite aspects of our start-up experience – the camaraderie and real-time decision making.

On the other hand, I also think it's an important part of showing the value of leadership. As we have grown over the years, my role has moved away from developing processes and running programmatic areas to being more of a guardian of our vision, mission and values, ensuring that our employees, partners, but especially the newest members of our community, understand why they are there and the role that they need to play.

As part of this, I have made it a priority to have a meal and conversation with every single one of our new teachers each summer. On each occasion, I try to model the values of integrity and collaboration by encouraging them to ask me any questions they would like, but I always start the meal by asking them to introduce themselves and tell me why they joined Teach First. Partly, this is a way for me to keep my ear to the ground – but also, years later I often meet our participants and ambassadors in their schools, places of work at Teach First events or even in public – and it's much easier for us to chat if we've already had a conversation. (This has sometimes backfired. I was once taking a shower in my municipal gym when one of our teachers noticed me and greeted me with excitement. As I tried to shampoo, he sidled up to me to complain about some of the decisions his headteacher had made in his school. It was a moment where I did feel I needed a bit more personal space.)

In the early years, these meals were relatively easy undertakings as our group of 200 could be polished off in ten or so dinners of about twenty people each. However, in recent years, as we've grown to an intake of a thousand, it has proven logistically more difficult – involving double or triple dinners, breakfasts and lunches throughout the six-week summer institute.

Yet, it has continued to be a crucial part of reminding me that Britain actually can "do" movements. The desire of young people – all people, really – to do noble things and have greater meaning in their lives is a strong one. In our modern, commercial and (in Britain) largely atheistic world, many people struggle to find this meaning. The ability to become part of a movement that makes the country a better place – by helping children get the education they need to be successful – is something that provides a powerful impetus for members of our community.

During the summer of 2011, as I attended one of the thirty-eight introduction meals, one of the women in the group gave me a particularly heartrending answer to my question of why she had joined Teach First. She had felt that she had to join us because Teach First had done so much for her. She had grown up in a low-income family and when she was a teenager at one of our partner schools, she had never thought that university was an option for her. It was the unrelenting mentoring and support of a Teach First ambassador, as well as the academic pressure from a number of our other teachers, that convinced her to apply to a top university, helping her through every stage of the application. Those teachers had changed her life and she wanted to change those of others. Amazingly, unbeknownst to her, the teacher who had mentored her university choices had since joined the Teach First staff team and was actually sitting a few rooms away. I made the introduction and witnessed a tear-jerking reunion.

During the early years of Teach First, we noticed that a large number of our teachers were taking up this sort of mentoring off their own backs. Whenever I asked the participants what their biggest surprise was in their teaching, they would answer something along the lines of this: that some of the students they were teaching were more insightful and dedicated than many of their friends at university had been; yet only a few of those same students were considering applying to university, and even fewer to the top universities away from their home towns. The latest research from the Sutton Trust seems to bear this out, noting that less than one student in a hundred admitted to Oxbridge between 2005 and 2007 had been eligible for free school meals.[6] This is not just the universities' fault. Of the 30,000 pupils who gained three A's at A-level in 2007/8, just 179 were getting free meals during that time. Our ambassadors know that this has to change if the children we work with are to get the opportunities they deserve.

6. Sutton Trust, "Responding to the New Landscape for University Access", December 2010.

Based on this desire from our community, we started a new initiative, which has the unfortunate acronym HEAPS – standing for the "Higher Education Access Programme for Schools". What started as a temporary name has stuck for six years now, difficult to change because of all the stakeholders involved. It's a good lesson on the importance of strategic naming!

As part of the initiative, we ask our teachers to identify children in their schools who come from low-income backgrounds, who do not have parents or carers with university experience, but crucially have shown the academic aptitude to get into Britain's best universities.

Each of the students gets an ambassador or Teach First employee mentor to work with them over an eighteen-month period, helping with university applications and choices. The highlight is a one-week residential course at Cambridge or another top university, where many of them realise that such places are not inhabited by aliens from other planets, but instead may be suitable for them. In six years, over 450 have completed their two years of being mentored, 76% of whom have already gone on to university. It has also helped to widen the movement to address educational disadvantage, as more and more students who are alumni of HEAPS help recruit for Teach First as our brand managers on campus and, now, are even joining us as teachers – creating a wonderful virtuous circle.

Most of our ambassadors have stayed in teaching – a larger percentage than we had originally expected. Ten years in, more than two-thirds of our ambassadors are still working in education, with the vast majority in teaching or leadership roles in schools in challenging circumstances.

Hundreds have also moved into middle or senior leadership roles in schools in challenging areas and we are beginning to see them play a larger role in the transformation of their schools.

In addition to all of the work that our ambassadors are doing with schools and pupils, they have also contributed to a societal shift. In the words of Chris Husbands, the director of the University of London's Institute of Education, Teach First has helped to "detoxify teaching for Britain's most talented graduates" and more specifically, he said, they have detoxified the idea of teaching in a school in challenging circumstances.

What is even more difficult to measure is how they are starting to change the national conversation. A national business leader who supports Teach First recently told me about a bizarre conversation at a social event he attended with a number of national politicians, CEOs and well-known journalists where the discussion normally would have centred around sport and gossip. Instead, they were talking knowledgeably about the situation in low-income schools and some of the successes of the children in them based on the personal familiarity they had gained from relatives and godchildren on the Teach First programme. In addition to the other facets of our community's impact, this is breaking down barriers and ensuring that people in the greatest position to make change happen are recognising the problem and discussing possible solutions.

In November 2007, we celebrated our fifth anniversary with a conference at the cavernous Excel Centre in east London. Over 500 of our teachers, ambassadors, supporters and employees came together in what felt like the greatest example of a movement yet. It was electrifying as dozens of the ambassadors and their colleagues led sessions on the work they were doing, including "High impact lesson ideas", "Leaders and dealers in hope" and "Addressing the needs and wants of learners".

It was a great day, as so many members of our community celebrated our success, but I felt strangely uneasy. When people approached me to offer congratulations and suggested that I must be incredibly happy with what we had achieved, I nodded, but for some reason couldn't share their sentiment. As hundreds of us retired to the pub and I was bought round after round, I actually felt lonelier than ever.

I walked most of the way home, unsure of the reasons for my reaction. It should have been one of the greatest days of my career. Why didn't it feel that way?

We had managed to put on a great party, but what impact exactly were we celebrating? We had continued to work with about a hundred schools and 200 to 250 new teachers each year. Our teachers and ambassadors were doing well, some outstandingly so, but, if we were being honest, were they really making enough change happen? We were no longer a start-up, but were still organisationally fragile.

The truth was that we were operating in controlled chaos most of the time, with poorly designed internal systems. A panic continued to come over me on the twentieth of each month as I checked our bank account to ensure we had enough to cover the payroll. Was this all that we could become? Was it our goal to just be a small part of the British educational establishment, working with a small number of young people, making marginal change and helping to keep things ticking over? While we put on a great party, I knew that we hadn't really scratched the surface of addressing educational disadvantage and we weren't doing a good enough job in stressing the sense of urgency that was necessary to support a real national movement that would change lives.

At the same time, the leadership of the organisation was lacking – starting with me. I was just beginning to get the hang of leading a small start-up and it wasn't clear that I could make the transition to lead the bigger, more professional organisation we needed to become in order to help catalyse large-scale change. I still struggled to manage through others and focused too much on process rather than people. My diary was a shambles as I ran from meeting to meeting, having to be involved in every decision and operational discussion, unable to delegate or success-fully empower large areas of the organisation.

It felt like Teach First had reached a plateau, as perhaps, had I. I had never planned to get involved in education, or to start a charity, and had never really thought through what I wanted to do when I "grew up". One thing was for sure – I had never expected to spend many years in one role or one organisation. I had always believed that my career – like that of many of our participants – would be more varied. Perhaps my role in life would be that of a serial entrepreneur, taking the lessons from our early years and using them to start a series of new initiatives and then passing them over to safer pairs of hands who could take them to the next level. One of my mentors, who was the CEO of a large company put it to me straight: "Brett, you need to decide if you are the right person to take Teach First to the next level. You may not be. Very few people are able to make that transition. It takes a completely different way of working and mindset."

After thinking about it, and discussing it with Nicole and Dame Julia, I decided to take on this personal challenge. I knew that there was so much more that Teach First could achieve. I was less sure whether or not I could be the right person to get the organisation there, but saw that by focusing on our values, I could try to develop myself to become that leader as the next step in my own leadership journey.

Of course, to do so, we needed to develop a leadership structure within the organisation that existed far beyond me. Dame Julia agreed to help expand our trustee board to include more individuals who had experience with fast-growing organisations and soon recruited a deputy chair in the guise of John Rink, the former global managing partner of Allen & Overy law firm from 1993 to 2003. He had helped lead its international growth from a small number of overseas offices to a truly global law firm, increasing both turnover and profit by 600%.

We also needed additional experienced leaders who could join Sonia Blandford, James Darley and Sarah Connor to help take us to the next stage of our development. I had already started to look further afield. In 2005, I had attended the fifteenth anniversary conference of Teach For America in Washington DC where one of their alumni who had been in a leadership role in the organisation, Amanda Timberg, approached me. Amanda had been a part of Teach For America's rapid growth in the previous five years and was interested in doing some international work. At that stage she was working for the Los Angeles School District and was thinking about her next step. She had worked extensively with schools and universities, experience which would fill a real gap on our staff. At the end of our coffee together, I asked her to come and lead our expansion outside of London and she soon agreed; she has since opened our second office in Manchester and brought in some much-needed additional expertise.

In early 2008, a few months after our anniversary event, we held another one of our annual offsites and I gave a call to arms in a strategy document given to our employees and trustees to mark this new beginning for us, trying to inject a renewed sense of urgency:

We could comfortably say that we have largely achieved the goals set out in our original 2002 business plan. Yet, when we look at the mission we are all working to achieve, we cannot say that we have achieved enough. The greatest determinant of a child's academic success in England remains the wealth of their parents. The children in our schools cannot wait for long-term results. Every year that goes by without the problem of educational disadvantage being fully addressed means there are additional children from low-income communities who lose their one and only chance to gain the life opportunities available from participating in a high quality education.

We have an obligation to do more and do it quicker in order to minimise these lost opportunities. We also believe based on the successes of our first five years, that there is a great deal more we can do with others to achieve these goals. Now is the time to look forwards.

In 2012, Teach First will be celebrating its 10th anniversary. What do we need to have achieved by this date in order to feel we have had a role in making a measurable impact on reducing this achievement gap and in addressing educational disadvantage?

The team who was there took this challenge on and, in the months afterwards, developed and launched our "2012 Mission Impact Strategy", which tried to define what we wanted Teach First to look like on our tenth anniversary. This contained four main areas of focus:

1. To work with four times as many children, by growing in scale from around 200 teachers joining us each year, to over 800 teachers a year, becoming a national programme throughout England and starting to work in primary schools, while also maintaining the quality and consistency of the cohort we are recruiting.

2. To support all of our teachers to set and achieve goals for their pupils' educational achievement, access and aspirations that go beyond national expectations.

3. To create a real long-term movement, ensuring that Teach First Ambassadors are mobilised, equipped and inspired to address the Teach First mission as leaders in all fields through clear pathways in excellent teaching, school leadership, social entrepreneurship, charity and policy work,

and in the for-profit sector.

4. To transition the charity from a shaky start-up footing to a more sustainable organisation with strong processes that are underpinned by our values – investing in building world-class human resource, IT, finance, facility and governance functions.

There was mixed reaction as the full scale of this ambition was digested. Many members of our community were nervous and had justifiable concerns. We were, in the words of one of our supporters, "just a small peanut of a charity" that was struggling to survive month to month, living in a donated cabin without even a head of HR, much less any good organisational processes in place. Was it hubris to set such ambitious goals for such a short time frame? Some of our ambassadors worried that we would have to lower our standards if we were to grow to this scale – we would not seem as special as we were and the feeling of community would be lost. Others worried about how we would balance our core focus on ensuring our teachers were leaders with our push to help our participants set more meaningful classroom goals, not always seeing that these goals were the ultimate results of that leadership. Finally, there was the question of money. We had no financial reserves and had struggled to raise sufficient funds in the past – how would we pay for this newly ambitious strategy?

In the end, though, through the value of leadership from, not just me, but also some of our most vocal ambassadors, trustees and employees, we managed to re-orient Teach First onto this new trajectory.

It taught me a valuable lesson that ambition can actually feed on itself and start a positive cycle. The strategy enabled us to attract great staff members who were excited by it. They then also helped us attract the resources to fund this. As we communicated our goals, we found more and more organisations interested in supporting us, including many of the country's biggest corporations, professional service firms, charitable trusts and foundations. None of this would have happened if we hadn't continued to be ridiculously ambitious.

Around the same time as this strategic review, Gordon Brown had become Prime Minister and, with a prompting from Andrew Adonis, who was then Schools Minister, became interested in seeing how Teach First could work even more extensively across the country.

As I had learnt from experience, political leaders are often like lighthouses and when their beam flashes onto you, it can be sudden and blinding. On a Friday afternoon in October 2008, Dame Julia was in her holiday home on the Isle of Wight, while I was spending a weekend with friends renting a sailing boat off Portsmouth. As I relaxed on the deck with a beer, I suddenly received an urgent call. Dame Julia had just heard from 10 Downing Street that the Prime Minister wanted to make an announcement on social mobility the following Monday and include a mention of Teach First's expansion in the speech.

Unlike the Budget Speech in 2006, however, this time we were prepared and coordinated enough to be able to lift and twirl like Torville and Dean. Dame Julia and I worked furiously all weekend, me on the boat sailing in and out of phone reception with increasingly annoyed friends. There were hurried conference calls with Downing Street, Andrew and various civil servants to agree budgets and forms of wording that everyone could support. By the end of the weekend, we had agreed a way forwards. The Prime Minister would make an announcement about our national expansion, backed up by some financial support from the department, which we would then need to extend through additional private support.

By the time of the 2010 national election, this support was echoed in all three main party manifestos. The Liberal Democrats wrote, "We support the expansion of Teach First to attract more top graduates into teaching." The Conservatives undertook to "expand Teach First", while the Labour manifesto promised that "Teach First will be extended to attract more of the best graduates into teaching, including teaching in primary schools." We were the only charity mentioned approvingly by all three major national parties. With the also crucial support of growing numbers of business, foundation and individual philanthropic donors, we continued our ambitious national expansion beyond Manchester, Birmingham and Nottingham, to open offices in Bristol, Kent, Leeds and Newcastle.

Around the time of our fifth anniversary, the movement also became global. For years I had been approached by international visitors who were interested in finding out more about Teach First to see if they could create a similar organisation in their own countries. However, the difficulty of overcoming domestic opposition had overwhelmed them and none had managed to take it forwards. This first changed in 2006 when an Estonian social entrepreneur with a proven track record of success, Artur Taevere, came into our office to find out more about how Teach First operated. He soon co-founded a local adaptation called *Noored Kooli* (Youth to School) based in Tallinn. Soon entrepreneurs from Germany, Latvia and Lithuania approached us with similar questions and the Australian Deputy Prime Minister called for the creation of a programme based on "the Teach First model in the UK" in her own country.

My team were getting overwhelmed with requests from social entrepreneurs and government officials for information. As we were trying to figure out the best way to support this exciting development, I approached Wendy Kopp at Teach For America, who had also been contacted by entrepreneurs in countries as diverse as Chile and India, asking her similar questions about how they could learn from the Teach For America model to address the problem of educational inequity in their own contexts. Wendy and I decided to work together to see how we could support this burgeoning wider movement without taking away from the pure domestic focus of each of our own charities.

After a year of thinking through various design options, we launched a new organisation in September 2007 at the Clinton Global Initiative in New York City, with Bill Clinton and Tony Blair announcing the launch of this new Anglo-American partnership.

Called Teach For All, this global network has since expanded to include more than twenty-five partners around the world. These independent, locally governed and locally funded charities are working towards a common vision that all children in their countries will have the opportunity to attain an excellent education. Teach For All then works to increase and accelerate their impact by sharing the expertise that exists across the network, enabling all members to benefit from each other's knowledge and experience.

In the past five years, I have spent about a fifth of my time supporting Teach For All and its network of partners. As part of this, I have been lucky enough to witness extraordinary leadership in more than a dozen countries on five continents that is helping to ensure that more and more children globally receive the education they need. The greatest thing I have learned is that the similarities between even the most diverse cultures can far outweigh any differences. Leadership truly is an international skill and children in challenging circumstances in all countries need more of it.

While working for Teach For All, I have met some of the most impressive social entrepreneurs who have awed me with their ability to overcome much more difficult and entrenched bureaucracies and hurdles than I faced on my relatively easy ride in Britain; great staff members who have given up high paying private sector jobs to build movements that will change their countries; and hundreds of impressive teachers who are leaders in the widest variety of situations imaginable.

However, my most memorable observations have been in the classrooms. This has included young people packed onto tiny benches in Karachi learning English, children in Chile setting clear goals for their futures and what they need to do to achieve them, and Melbourne students moving from a bottom set class to among the highest achieving results in their schools.

The revolution has truly gone global.

When we went on our first milk round back in 2003, one of the messages we gave was to "join the revolution that will take a generation". We knew from the start that this was far more than a two-year programme. We always thought of it as a movement, even if we did not articulate it well. And that was always part of the attraction of joining: we were not just asking people to teach for two years. We were asking them to transform Britain and ensure all children had access to the education they needed – a powerful call to arms.

When I addressed our first summer institute, I told them that I believed that in twenty years' time their group would be great teachers, entrepreneurs, headteachers, business and government leaders – but united as national change agents who would work with great colleagues and the wider community to help ensure every child had access to an excellent education.

As Mao once said, "A revolution is not a dinner party, or writing an essay, or painting a picture, or doing embroidery." It is difficult and requires a sustained commitment.

There are no silver bullets. To reach our vision will take decades. It will take the leadership of thousands of individuals from both within and outside of Teach First. It will take the enduring belief that there's always a higher hill of happiness still to come. But like Edmund Hillary and Tenzing Norgay's ascent of Mount Everest, even the seemingly most impossible of climbs can become just a long and difficult path that hasn't yet been completely navigated.

This long-term perspective is important, not least because we are only part way there. It's like building a house. To start, we laid the plans and built the foundations. People may have believed that we were just digging a hole. But we knew the truth. We were building the future: the more secure the foundations, the better the building.

We do not expect all of our people to be incredibly effective teachers, great school leaders or transformational system leaders from the beginning, but we do expect them to work within the value of leadership to increase their effectiveness every year until they get there. They are massing and more and more will start to break through in the next few years, joining others from outside of Teach First who share in our common vision. A benevolent tsunami of leadership is about to wash away generations of educational inequity. It's the only thing that can.

HOW TO SCRAP THE GAP
A dream of Britain in 2022

Over the past decade, I have come to the conclusion that successful classes, charities and companies have a number of things in common.

- They focus on a clear and inspiring mission.
- They have common values that inform everyone how to work towards this mission.
- They have a clear and achievable strategy that underpins their work, with measurable goals to show them if they've been successful.

By our eighth anniversary in 2010, we were working within these frameworks and, in many ways, were well on track to achieve most of the main pillars of the "2012 Mission Impact Strategy" (recruiting more great teachers, training them successfully, engaging ambassadors in the mission and building a sustainable organisation). However, during some conversations with employees, participants, ambassadors and supporters, I realised that we were in danger of losing sight of the real essence of the work we were trying to do. We had become so focused on achieving certain measurable goals (recruit X number of teachers), that we had sometimes forgotten the underlying reason behind the work (to help children have the life chances they deserved).

We needed to pivot away from being seen as "just" a graduate recruiter or a teacher trainer. We needed to get back to first principles by refocusing on our ultimate goal – to address educational disadvantage. I asked one of our employees who was a former McKinsey consultant, Rania Marandos, to lead a process over the next eighteen months that would enable Teach First to develop a strategy for our second decade.

The process has gone through the following steps:

1. Refocus on our "primary beneficiaries"

The first thing we had to do was refocus everyone on the charity's "primary beneficiaries": the schoolchildren in challenging circumstances that Teach First was set up to serve. During our annual employee offsite, we kicked this off with an "I have a dream" session where every one of our staff members expressed his or her dream for the British educational system.

I then made the most unlikely decision of the process – to uproot the entire middle and senior leadership team, as well as our chair and deputy chair (about twenty-five people in total), to Mumbai and Pune to spend a week with our sister organisation, Teach For India, as a dramatic way to press the reset button and refocus ourselves directly on the problem of educational disadvantage. At first, many people were surprised by this idea – was it a good use of our charitable resources and our employees' time to travel half way around the world? But, the truth was that, since we shared rooms in very inexpensive local hotels, the cost was less than a short strategic retreat in Britain and I was confident that there was nowhere that we could learn more from. This trip was crucial for us. We needed to develop "new eyes" in order to reorient our strategy and remove any complacency we might have.

I had met the CEO of Teach For India, Shaheen Mistri, the previous year at a Teach For All conference and was impressed with her inspiring belief in what was possible for her teachers to accomplish with children in even the most impoverished communities. I believed that for us to truly dream an impossible dream for Great Britain, we needed to step out of the day-to-day execution of our roles and understand how Teach For India was keeping the dream alive in a very different and challenging educational context. It also was an opportunity for us to analyse our own strengths and weaknesses; and bond as the Teach First leadership team needed to take the organisation forwards to climb the next, much higher, hill in front of us.

Teach For India generously supported us in this endeavour. We spent three days with their staff, teachers and the children they served in some of the most difficult slum communities in Mumbai and Pune. We saw inspiring classes where the teachers led ten-year-old children, who were learning English as a third language, to engage in complicated debates on Gandhi's values, to compete in book reading competitions where the winners showed us listsof books they had read that ran into triple digits, and to perform Shakespeare's plays. Children who would then return home to a tiny concrete room lacking modern sanitation that they shared with their extended families. On the last day of the trip, we regrouped to decide how we wanted Teach First to change as a result of this visit. The team immediately agreed – the organisation needed to be more clearly focused on the children we were serving, and we needed to raise our sense of what was possible for them.

2. Define and articulate our vision for them

This led to us thinking even more about what success could look like. We had used our mission to help focus our strategy for the better part of a decade, but there were often frustrations that it wasn't always clear what "addressing educational disadvantage" meant. It was too vague and could be shorthand for anything. We needed a simple statement that could unite us around a common goal. Cancer Research UK's vision is that "together we will beat cancer"; Make Poverty History's was "to end extreme poverty". What was ours?

Through a collaborative process, we agreed that, in our view, the ultimate success for our movement in the UK would be a country where "no child's educational success is limited by their socio-economic background".

This was a powerful statement of intent and has proven inspirational and clarifying for many members of our community. However, I worried it could be too ephemeral to actually influence our work. While it was a laudable dream, we knew that it could take generations to achieve. It would be too easy to put this vision on a shelf somewhere, confident that a future generation would make it happen. How could we know in a shorter time-frame if we were helping to nudge things in the right direction towards this boldly ambitious end-goal?

3. Develop measurements to determine if progress is being made towards this vision over the next ten years

This led to the development of what we call our "National Impact Goals", to clarify what success really looks like – time-limited, measurable data points that could be collected annually to help us know if the children we were looking to serve were better off, or if we were just spinning our wheels.

This ended up becoming the longest, and possibly most important, part of the process. We spent the better part of a year having conversations with a broad range of stakeholders about how they would define success in this area as well as what needed to happen across society to close the gaps. Included in these conversations were our headteachers, policy and charity leaders, global educational experts and our participants and ambassadors (including a 1,000-person brainstorming session that we held during the 2011 summer institute).

Some of the conversations were highly philosophical (what is the goal of education?), while others tested our thinking around what was possible (should children in our schools work towards a minimum threshold, or towards closing the gap with more affluent children?). They all served to move our thinking forwards and have led to five measurable National Impact Goals for England and Wales. These define what we mean by educational success for children in low-income communities and ensure that the movement of leaders working to address educational disadvantage is more focused on what needs to be achieved. Each one has actual numerical goals attached to it. They are:

- Narrow the gap in literacy and numeracy at primary school.
- Narrow the gap in GCSE attainment at secondary school.
- Ensure pupils develop key strengths, including resilience and wellbeing, to support high aspirations.
- Narrow the gap in the proportion of pupils in education, employment or training one year after compulsory education.
- Narrow the gap in university graduation, including from the 25% most selective universities.

The consultation also emphasised the many interventions that are required across society to enable children from low-income families to succeed (within the classroom, school and community, as well as the wider system). This then led to a central tenet of our strategy: there is no one solution to educational disadvantage; a movement of leaders from across society needs to work together towards this common vision.

4. Identify what Teach First's role is in supporting this progress over the coming years and define the organisational goals that will enable us to know whether or not we are successful in this strategy

We were able to use this process to determine what the most important contribution was that "Teach First" could make to support this wider movement over the next decade. This has led to us agreeing to three areas of focus for the coming years, while continuing to ensure we strengthen as an organisation:

- Increasing the number and impact of Teach First participants and ambassadors
- Building collective impact towards the vision from outside this community

- Testing innovative ways of addressing educational disadvantage (both to share externally and also to feed into our future strategy)

We have then drilled down to specific annual organisational goals for Teach First under these headings, while also understanding that the wider movement will continue to develop their own ways to work towards the end vision. The organisational goals will drive how we allocate our resources over the next three years, as well as underpin the objectives each employee will set for themselves.

Of course, phrases like "vision", "mission", "national impact goals" and "strategy" are just words that can easily deteriorate into mumbo-jumbo. As a management consultant, I saw many organisations go through the process of developing all of these things, but then not successfully making the structural and cultural changes necessary for them to be really meaningful. For this to really work, it has to permeate the roots of the organisation and not just be a quick process run by a few senior members of staff in a dark room. This was even more crucial for our work, as a core part of our impact is influencing the wider movement of ambassador leaders that we are trying to support. The process we went through – including the trip to India, a long period of wide consultations, and regular strategic communications – has hopefully ensured that we will have a solid foundation to increase our impact for our second decade of operation, helping more children realise ever increasing levels of success in their educational achievements, life aspirations and access to opportunities.

CONCLUSION

During the summer of 2010, Jouman, a teenager at one of our partner schools in west London, spent a fortnight on work experience supporting me in our head office. On his return to school, he wrote me a thank you note that I have kept at my desk as a personal inspiration and a reminder of the lessons I have learned while building a values-based organisational culture.

Brett – The time I've spent at Teach First proved an amazing one. The environment within is very comforting and you all seem like a family. I've been very humbled by your mission to address educational disadvantage and have seen all the hard work, passion and care you put into your work as a team even if times are hard and stressful. I'm sure because of your busy schedule that you don't see yourself first-hand the impact you've had on the schools, but I assure you, from what I've seen in schools, particularly mine, there is exponential growth down to the Teach First teachers. Their skills have all come from the core. For that I'd like to thank the whole Teach First team.

I can only ask one thing of you and Teach First: I hope you continue with your mission to combat educational disadvantage. I think you have the right group of people with the right attitude and mentality. All I can say is that the teachers you introduce to these schools are different and unique, for all the right reasons. I hope we keep in touch.

The only way poverty of aspirations will end and all of our children's life chances improve is if there is a radical change in the national reality that forces some children and their communities to believe that educational success is something for others – not for them.

In decades past, there have been a number of truths that many people were confident would never change:

- Slavery is natural and an economic necessity
- Women are not decision makers and therefore cannot be trusted with the vote
- A man of African descent can never be President of the United States
- Protestants and Catholics in Northern Ireland can never peacefully share power
- A child's education success is normally limited by their socio-economic background

In previous decades, all of these myths have been shattered, except one.

The future doesn't have to be like the present, just as

252

the present doesn't have to be like the past. Two of the lessons of history are that change is possible and that most people think it is impossible.

Just one decade ago, there were also a number of truths that many people were confident about:

- This will never get started
- You are the wrong person to lead it
- Top graduates will never teach in those schools
- Training them to teach those children will be impossible
- Britain doesn't "do" movements

Yet, over the past ten years, each one of these certainties has been demolished. Using the values of Commitment, Integrity, Excellence, Collaboration and Leadership, thousands of Teach First colleagues have proven that change can happen.

In 2002, few of the UK's top graduates considered teaching in a school in challenging circumstances as a viable career choice. Many of these schools struggled to recruit enough high-quality teachers, had relatively low expectations of their pupils and regularly failed to have more than 25% of their pupils gain five good GCSEs. For these reasons, most pupils from low-income backgrounds suffered the double disadvantage of being a poor pupil in a poor school and were consequently limited from achieving the same levels of educational success as their wealthier peers.

Yet, in 2012, many classrooms, departments and schools across the country, led by incredibly focused and inspirational headteachers and senior leaders, are changing as Teach First participants and ambassadors and their colleagues make a real measurable impact in the educational aspirations and achievement of their pupils. A powerful social change movement is being created with thousands of Britain's best graduates working together to focus everyone's energies to ensure all children are able to receive the education that will allow them to make the most of their abilities.

During the original McKinsey study in 2002, the team was unable to find any schools in London in challenging circumstances that matched the national average of 47% of children gaining five or more good GCSEs at 'C' grade or above. The academic results in London schools, with their larger percentage of children from low-income families, were measurably below the national average.[7] However, within ten years, London has become the only capital city in Europe doing better than its national average – over 62% of its state-school educated children achieved at least five GCSEs at 'C' grade or above (including English and Maths), compared with 58% in the rest of the UK. Some have pushed far past it, with at least eight of those serving the lowest-income communities ensuring that more than 75% of their children gained this benchmark.[8]

There are many reasons for London's improvement, including some policy changes and hard work from a number of great headteachers, middle leaders and class-

7. The London Challenge, "Transforming London Secondary Schools" Department for Education and Skills, 2003

8. The mayor's education inquiry, first report, London context and call for evidence, February 2012

room teachers throughout the city, much of which was instigated through the London Challenge initiative, led by Professor Tim Brighouse under the last government. Such changes provide powerful examples of what is possible with effective leadership and an ambitious sense of possibility. As a result of these changes, thousands of children from low-income backgrounds have moved onto elevated life trajectories.

Even as some improvements take place, though, it is still the case that in 2012, educational disadvantage remains one of the most destructive and pervasive problems we face. The achievement gap between pupils of different socio-economic backgrounds is larger in the UK than in most developed countries in the world.[9]

There are still schools across the country which are undeniably failing the children that they serve. When I recently asked one headteacher in the West Midlands if he thought any of his students would move on to university, he looked at me sceptically. "University? These children's lives are the square mile around this council estate. There's only so much we can do." He walked me out with a shrug of his shoulders and a closing comment that he meant as friendly banter, but has stuck with me ever since. "You have to understand, Brett, it doesn't matter how much you polish a piece of coal – you'll never get a diamond out of it."

So seemingly obvious to him, yet so untrue.

So many other great teachers and school leaders across the country know the reality that it is possible to succeed

9. Department for Education, "How Does the Social Attainment Gap in England Compare with Countries Internationally?" PISA 2009.

against the odds. There are diamonds that exist in every single one of their schools – in every single one of their students – just waiting for their opportunity to shine.

In more and more of the schools that I visit, I no longer see failure with a few tiny pockets of inspiration. Instead, I see growing belief in the power of teachers as classroom leaders to change the lives of young people. I see the beginnings of real societal change and the possibility of fundamentally rewriting the social contract throughout Great Britain.

**

As part of our tenth anniversary, I decided to return to Chris's school in west London where it had all started a decade earlier. I could feel a knot in my stomach as I passed the same landmarks. The local council estate was the same as ever, in the midst of an even more depressed economic reality.

I went into a classroom. Just as there had been years before, an argument was going on. This time it was about Dickens, more specifically his use of allegory. As the class finished, I went to one of the tables and asked the students what they were working on. A new argument commenced. "Our English GCSEs," they replied. "We're going to get As or A*s." One boy disagreed. "Maybe you're all getting A's, but I'm not. I'm getting a C." He was shouted down by his peers before he gave them a toothy grin. "OK, OK, I'm just joking. What do you think this is? I'm not about to be the dumbest person here! No way am I going to be the one to let the class down!"

What's changed in this school?

Unlike ten years ago, they haven't been given up on

by the people responsible for their success. Their teachers are working within the values of commitment, integrity, excellence, collaboration and leadership to help the young people get to a place that they might never have thought possible for themselves.

In the past ten years, their school has brought in a new headteacher, new governors, some new building work. But, the headteacher would say that the greatest influence has been the work of her teachers, all of them, new and experienced, who have believed in the children and worked hard to make that belief a new reality. They have changed the mood and ethos of the place by refusing to accept failure and instead seizing their incredible responsibility.

This is not a unique story. These children are no different than other young people – they are just lucky enough to be surrounded by adults who believe it is their role to help them shine. This school is just one of dozens around the country who show that change can take place and children from all backgrounds can be successful – as long as it's our priority. And, it has to be. It really does.

The bell rang and all the students gathered up their things. I asked one of the boys, Paul, what he planned to do next. He looked at me sheepishly. "Well, truth is, I don't even like English you know. I prefer Maths. I want to go on and study Engineering at Imperial or Manchester, I think those are the two best unis that do it. Mr Hussain [another Teach First teacher] is getting me ready for A-level Maths next year, but I'm going to have to do Further Maths [A-level] as well if I want a chance to get a place there."

Impressed, I asked Paul if he had seen any changes in the school during his five years there. He laughed. "Ermm, yeah!" He replied with a tone of incredulity that only a teenager could muster. "This place is way different now. It was still a mess back when I started and only a few people cared." He paused. "Actually, it was really bad for a long time. My brother used to go here and the stories he used to tell me... Gosh... Mad!"

I asked him what his brother was doing now and almost instantly regretted it. Paul seemed to shrink in front of me and looked down at the floor, shrugging his shoulders. "Nothing much. He gets into trouble a lot, I guess."

Paul turned to head off with his mates, but something held him back. He stopped and looked back at me, his eyes suddenly burning with a sense of anger that I hadn't seen up until then. "You know, it's crazy because my brother is actually the smart one! He just never got a chance. That's out of order. Isn't it?"

Isn't it?

ACKNOWLEDGEMENTS

So many people provided support for this book that it was the best possible example of the value of collaboration. I'd especially like to thank Hannah Essex, Rania Marandos, Jo Owen, Amanda Timberg and Rachel Wasser who provided detailed edits and advice, as well as James Westhead who also shepherded me through the entire publishing process and urged me on. Great thanks must also go to Teach First's indomitable chair Dame Julia Cleverdon and our board of trustees for their support.

This book would not have been possible without the patience of my wife, Nicole, and children Noa, Gilad and "Wiglet", as well as my amazing assistant Jo Lee who found me blocks of time and quiet places to write in areas as far flung as Abu Dhabi, Canterbury, East Finchley, Edinburgh, New York City, Newcastle, Norfolk, Lensbury, Southwark and Tel Aviv. I was also inspired by all of the great educators in my family, including my mother, brother and all my many aunts, uncles and cousins in the profession.

Thanks also to Keith and Helen Rose in Booton, Norfolk, who allowed me to spend time in their farmhouse and cooked delicious dinners to facilitate the writing process.

I very much appreciate the time and expertise of all of the following individuals who have provided advice, guidance and feedback on key passages of the text: Lord Andrew Adonis, Gill Bal, Luisa Barile, Professor Sonia Blandford, Anesta Broad, Nick Canning, Ruth Carney, Dame Julia Cleverdon, John Colenutt, Zaki Cooper, James Darley, Louise Davies, Neela Dolezal, Hannah Essex, Laura Feeney, Simon Gallagher, Shelley Gonsalves, Flora Grimston, Max Haimendorf, Maggie Hughes, Walter Isaacson, Matt Lloyd, Rania Marandos, Hannah McCullagh, Katy Miller, Reuben Moore, Professor John Moss, Vanessa Ogden, Ndidi Okezie, Jo Owen, Sanju Pal, Briony Phillips, Katherine Richardson, John Rink, Anthony Seldon, Matt Sheldon, Professor Ralph Tabberer, Artur Taevere, Amanda Timberg, Professor Dylan Wiliam and Teach First's leadership development team who developed our philosophy on leadership detailed in the relevant text box. And thanks to the wonderful team at Short Books for all their work.

Finally, there have been literally hundreds of individuals who have been crucial to our success, but are unfortunately unnamed in the book. It would have been impossible to include everyone responsible for getting Teach First to its current stage or who have helped along the way. So many wonderful headteachers, educators, business leaders, philanthropists, policy makers, mentors and influencers showed the leadership just when it was needed. I just hope they know how much they are appreciated. Thank you.

Brett Wigdortz has led Teach First as its CEO since its launch in July 2002. He is also the co-founder and chief strategy advisor of Teach For All. Before coming to London, he worked for McKinsey & Company in Indonesia, Singapore and the Philippines, the Asia Society in New York City and the East-West Center in Honolulu. He was recently named UK Social Entrepreneur of the Year. He is married with two small children. He can be followed on Twitter at @wigdortz.